THE LONG WAY HOME

Shawn,
  Thank you for being such a good friend.
  You are a wonderful individual & Christlike example of love and caring!
I Corinthians Sincerely,
              Clee Emery Pugh

THE LONG WAY HOME

One woman's true story of a love lost and another one found

CLARA EMERY PUGH

Carpenter's Son Publishing

The Long Way Home: One Woman's True Story of a Love Lost and Another One Found

Copyright © 2011 by Clara Pugh

Published by Carpenter's Son Publishing, 307 Verde Meadow Drive, Franklin, TN 37067

Published in association with Larry Carpenter of Christian Book Services, LLC
www.christianbookservices.com

Cover and Interior Layout Design: Frank Gutbrod

ISBN: 0-9832846-0-1
EAN: 978-0-9832846-0-4

Printed in the United States of America

All rights reserved.

INTRODUCTION

If my love, Marvin, had not come into my life, I'm quite certain that no book would have been written. Some of the incidents of the past were too unpleasant to recall and, therefore, I chose to bury them and walk away. But he changed all that. When others who knew me would hear about the Korean War that took his legs below the knees and the unbelievable miracles that saved his life, they urged me to write about our two lives.

Often times with tragedy, a tinge of humor would creep in. An example was his comment to the doctor in the military hospital in Japan who apparently dreaded to inform him his legs had to go. Nearby was another young Marine also with gangrene that had set in. The doctor walked about during the exams, and Marvin noticed his apprehensive mood. When he began the exam, Marvin blurted, "When are you going to take my legs off?" Startled, the doctor replied, "How did you know?" He answered, "They always cut gangrene legs off in the cowboy shows I seen back home."

During the night, the other young Marine died, but Marvin kept his appointment with the surgeon as daylight approached. He woke up during the preparation to feel the incision points being drawn on his legs. He spoke to the doctor to spare his knees, but the surgeon replied he would have to have a second operation later. Marvin adamantly insisted he would take that chance. When he awoke, the doctor had granted his request—Marvin still had and still has his knees.

It is refreshing to be with this man who so bravely served his country. He is not bitter, nor burdened with self pity. He goes through each day with courage, and a desire to do his best at whatever he tackles. It was not unusual to hear that he had done almost the impossible.

With prostheses on, he built many things. Among them are the library in his beloved Church, wooden boxes/holders for individual mail, another group for Church brochure and announcements and portable holders for flags and crosses.

Marvin also made the wooden holders for the banners (embroidered by the ladies of the Church) that depict the highlights of the Holy Scriptures. They hang from the narrow balconies on each side of the Nave.

I was told that he was constantly called upon by Father Peter Whalen and that these chores would have been willingly multiplied many times over if the Church secretary had not gently "scolded" him for working Marvin too much. This hard work apparently was his form of rehabilitation.

TRUE STORY

Never did I envision writing about my life, especially an entire book. But after much urging from those who conceived the thought, I began. After completing the manuscript (to be sure it was my story as I wrote it word-for-word), I sought a self-publishing connection.

Petey Richards, a trusted, and exceptionally personable member of our Church came to mind. As an owner of his own business, Teasley's Convention Florist of Nashville, I decided that he must know some things about how businesses operate. I approached him, explaining my wish to publish a totally true story, not fiction in any part, to give others possible hope to confront their problems with faith. If they could read about my constant battles to overcome the every day obstacles, the desire for peace and a tranquil life, they could see themselves also reaching that goal.

Petey talked to his friends in the printing industry, and they suggested Larry Carpenter, President and CEO of a company in nearby Franklin, Tennessee. Larry's company is Christian Book Services. How could I go wrong with a company with a name like that?

I called Larry and told him that I wanted to print a book in my own words, not edited for commercial appeal, and he granted my wishes. Thanks to his patience with me and his hard work, he accomplished what seemed like the impossible for me.

The Reverend Vicki Burgess gave me spiritual resolve. Two friends of my daughter were very helpful in the writing of the book. Wanda gave me courage after reading my manuscript. Linda wrote an overwhelming letter of appreciation for allowing her to read it, too. Some of her excerpts are as follows: "privilege to read...honest, true picture...This would make such a wonderful movie!... reminded me of what I have been missing...honesty and humor...the sacrifices you made!...Your book will be a huge success...great things you have accomplished...May God bless you and your husband, and THANK YOU for the shared blessing of your life story."

Comments such as these have made this project so dear to me. I hope you enjoy my book as much as Wanda and Linda!

Clara Emery Pugh

CHAPTER 1

This is our wedding day.

Marriage is supposed to be for life, with both of us doing our best to out-achieve the other in being the best mate.

Once my head was committed to this fidelity, my heart and intentions followed. There is no excuse for not giving my very best to my companion and love.

What else could be fair and acceptable, since we plan to spend our lifetime together?

This is about my beloved Marvin and me.

To this day, I don't understand how we met again. It had been 55 years since I remembered seeing him.

He said he was at my restaurant in the 70s, when I hosted our high school class of 1946, a reunion I remember, but not all the people who attended. This was many years ago, too.

In what ways did I remember him?

In high school, he was small-built, extremely handsome with thick black hair and black eyebrows, smiling slightly, with one arm slung over the library chair or leaning forward on both elbows watching the hall traffic.

His acknowledgment of me, as I remember, was always a casual "hi" and a faint gesture of his hand. He seemed to smile from the side of his mouth. I would smile and go on my way, nothing else.

Now, we are in St. Philip's Episcopal Church to be married.

This is Marvin's lifetime church. Though I had worshiped with almost every Christian denomination, it was he who brought me for my first visit to an Episcopal service.

Instead of a sermon during our marriage ceremony, Father Peter Whalen read the following poignant letter to Marvin, me, and those present for the wedding.

November 23, 2001

Dear Marvin and Clara,

I write this letter to you because today is such a special day—your wedding day.

I write this letter to you, because, in the midst of all that happens today, and of all the two of you do today, in the midst of all these good people—your family and friends—who come to be with you, nothing is more important than your desire to be here in this time and place, with this community of faith to proclaim publicly that you promise to be as good as God for each other. I admire your courage more than I admire your love because I believe that, before there can be true love, there must be true courage. Your individual lives have been stories of courage, over many years.

You begin with prayer. You understand that what you do here is far more than just for today, or for your personal convenience, or for the conventions of society. You undertake a noble purpose, which has no room for passing fancies, nursed wounds, power plays or bruised egos. Jesus says to you and all of us "love one another as I have loved you." Remain in my love. You want us to hear what you say to each other: "No matter what comes, I will love you. I will cherish you. I will honor you. No matter what comes... so help me God." That is bravery. I do not think that kind of courage comes easily—nor does it come to everyone. You two are fortunate. Do you understand? This is pure grace. I think you do understand. The joy of God will be yours and your joy will be complete when you live in His love.

I listened carefully as you told me your stories. Your faith and God's grace will be your strength to live out what you promise here today. It takes the very determination, which is at the heart of God's courage and love for you to live as Paul suggests—with sincerity, respect, perseverance, generosity, humility, mercy, kindness, patience, and thankfulness. On this day everybody else gives you gifts. Instead, I have a request to make of you. For as much as the promises you make today are to each other, please understand that you are making these promises to us, too.

You are the salt of the earth. We need to see your love withstand the strong, cold winds of division. We need to see your faithfulness prevail against the odds, as it has in your earlier lives. We need to see in your words and actions how human beings can be as good as God for one another.

You give us hope that, with Christ, we can live at peace with each other. Your relationship can encourage us in all of our trials. Will you always keep us in mind—not just your family and friends, but the people you will meet, the strangers you pass by on the street? We need you to show us the courage we must have to love as Christ did. If what you do here today is to have any meaning in the long history of the human race, then we need you.

Finally, Marvin and Clara, I want you to know you are in my humble prayer as the priest—intercessor who witnesses your vows together with this entire community. I love you, too, and I pray that God will always hold the two of you in the palm of His hand. That is a safe place to grow older together in your life.

Your friend, Peter

Wait! I'm getting too far ahead in my desire to get you to know my beloved, the love of my life. He insisted that if I was to write about him, the hero I have found him to be then I must tell my story, too; how I became the person that he loves. He insisted that I be first, I agreed only after I told him that I was saving the very best until last.

I was a precocious child, I guess, always wanting to lead. My parents already had seven children, when I came along. Two sisters in their preteens had died in the 1918 flu epidemic.

My mother, the daughter of a merchant, had come from a small Tennessee town.

From the bits of conversation I remember, there was always household help for my grandmother. Grandfather ruled with the last word, the only word. My mother said my grandmother addressed him as Mr. Lindsay at all times, never calling him by his first name nor ever raising her voice in rebuttal to anything he said or proposed in or out of the house.

Grandfather had a blacksmith shop, a store that sold groceries, dry goods, etc. and later added a saloon to his holdings. This did not remain open very long, because he did not like to see men frequent his business for liquor and, then as a result, not provide adequately for their wives and children.

When I grew older and could understand the whisperings and innuendos when my parents would argue, I learned that he had a child by one of the servants, and my grandmother reared him as her own, never bringing up to him or grandfather that he was not her child. Of course, after this boy was born, the birth mother left and was apparently never heard from again.

Since he was the final word on everything, after my grandmother's death he left all possessions and monies to his second wife. Explaining in the will I was to learn about in my recent years that my mother and siblings were married and old enough to provide for themselves, that the second wife was young, and the children by her were so young, they needed the inheritance. To my knowledge, no one ever questioned this decision. Grandfather was 65 and his new wife was 18 when they married. This was without a doubt, a May/December union.

My father was from a farm family. One of his brothers served in World War I, never married, stayed on the farm to help his parents, before and after the war.

There were other siblings, one whose family still owns the land they inherited, dating back to the original purchase from North Carolina. My father was told before he married that he was not to expect any inheritance if he left the farm after marrying, since he would not be there to share in working the land for my grandparents. Another tidbit that I would hear when my parents argued was my mother saying, "I thought you had something when I married you." I soon realized that my mother did not have her mother's disposition—my mother spoke her mind at all times.

Papa often spoke of the circuit rider that was the Methodist preacher. He and a schoolteacher stayed at my grandparents' farm, as the Church/schoolhouse was on their land.

I visited my parent's town a few years ago and saw a charming one-room schoolhouse in the middle of town and wondered if my mother had attended it at some time in her life.

The only known photo of my deceased eldest sisters was in a double oval tin frame, decorated with a long stemmed rose in the center. Alma's picture showed only her dress collar and her face; Lucy's was the same.

Following their births came my brother, Malcolm (Mac); my sister, Jennie; my sister, Donie; brother, James (Buster). He was nicknamed Buster because of something said by a cousin who took him during the flu epidemic of 1918 (that took my sisters, Alma and Lucy). To help convince my mother that he would return after the family recovered from the flu, she said, "When he returns, he will be a real buster (tough guy in those days)." Actually, my cousin thought she was taking him to die, to keep my mother from seeing him leave her as my sisters did.

Everyone in the family had the flu except for my father who was working at the powder plant (for WWI) in Old Hickory. He said men died on the job and makeshift caskets were stacked within the factory. No doctors were available; they were all so busy around the clock.

When cousin Lucy brought James home, they said he really was a "Buster." His legs were wrinkled with fat, and his cheeks were fat and rosy. I remember a picture, and he was truly a beautiful baby. Cousin Lucy and her daughters had spent entire nights nursing this sick baby, forcing him to take any nourishment that he could tolerate. This went on for weeks, as my other siblings fought to stay alive with no medical help. After they recovered, then cousin Lucy brought James home and declared triumphantly, "I told you I would bring back a real buster." From then on, he was seldom referred to as James, only as "Buster."

My parents had moved from their home town of Dover on a flatboat. They arrived in Nashville, where Buster was born, as was my brother, Roy. I was the eighth and last child. (Roy was five years older than I.)

Mama and Papa are buried in the town's church yard next to a civil war fort. In town, there is a former hotel in which my cousin, Violet, and I played when we were children. It was there a Confederate general surrendered to a Yankee general, so I was told. I still remember the path they said the general took to the hotel to accept surrender.

I fondly remember going to visit cousins in the summertime, walking the streets of crushed limestone in bare feet, going into that hotel unsupervised and marveling at the history of that area.

On the farms, one fun thing was to go across the road to the creek and bathe. As a small child, I would sit on an embankment and fish. My pole was a stick made from a tree branch, and the hook was a bent pin. Alone I would sit and believe that I was truly fishing. When I was not fishing, I was wading in the cool waters on a hot summer day, watching the minnows I could not seem to catch. Many fond memories are associated with those days.

CHAPTER 2

My father came home from work one night and during supper asked my mother and me if we would like to go to the carnival. We were climbing out of the Post Depression years and entertainment was at a premium. I remember the long walk (my father never learned to drive a car. We could not afford this luxury anyway, and neither could any of our neighbors). At that time, I was five years old.

We wandered around the carnival, my parents with a ho-hum attitude, but I was delighted at the crowds, the laughter, the merriment, the tents, the carnival garish atmosphere and loudness of the men barking their wares, and especially the belly dancers, girls with their flimsy costumes (well-covered according to today's standards); my mother only let me linger for a moment and grabbed my hand as I stared.

In moments we were in front of the minstrel tent. They both agreed that this would be entertaining and full of laughter.

Apparently, an entertainer in the show was late in arriving. The audience was getting restless. Someone began to play the piano. Another showman waved his hands for the pianist to stop. Then he announced that they were having a talent contest, with the prize being tickets to every show and every ride at the carnival.

The only ones with courage to go down seemed to be young people, as I recall. I said excitedly, "Mama, I want to go down there to sing."

"No," my mother replied, embarrassed that I should ask.

Papa said, "Oh, Delia, let her go!" He laughed and pushed me into the aisle.

The floors were of sawdust, and the stage was a hastily built wooden structure. I was, as I remember, the youngest contestant, and I was last in the line.

There was a drum roll by a very talented drummer; and the pianist seemed to have a storehouse of songs he could play.

After the other contestants finished tap dancing, singing, reciting, and whatever else, a round of applause followed each, and then I came up. I asked the pianist if he knew the song, "Goody, Goody." Of course, he did, and I began to sing and act as I did in front of my older siblings, who seemed delighted with my "shows" at home. When I got to various lyrics in the song I would act out what I thought was appropriate. "Goody, Goody for you." I pointed to people in the audience; they laughed. For the lyrics "...and I hope you're satisfied, you, Rascal, you!" I then angrily shook my finger at others. They laughed. Then I kicked my leg up high as a Rockette from Radio City. There was a standing ovation, and I had to sing it again—an encore. I looked at my parents. My father was smiling with delight, but my mother had her head down in embarrassment.

We left the tent, not staying for the show. I never learned if the musician or comic didn't show up or if my mother simply refused to stay. My first-place prize was the opportunity to ride or visit any offering of the carnival for free. Needless to say, my father found me amusing. I got to ride the horses (carousel) twice and others that were "tame" enough that I could ride alone.

Back home the next day, my friends treated me as though I had won the sweepstakes.

My parents were in their 40s when I was born. My nearest sibling, Roy, was mentally retarded. In North Nashville, the neighborhood children called him "Susie" as a nickname. Because he often wandered away, the only way my mother could keep him in the house was to put a dress on him. He was humiliated with a dress on, and the object of much teasing. My mother was afraid other people would hurt him, especially the other boys who wanted to pick fights with him, not understanding his "difference" in behavior. My mother shed many tears and was sad at the ridicule he suffered.

He had a severe speech impediment, pronouncing his words as a small child would. Also, he always started his sentences with "me want," "me like..." instead of "I want" or "I like..."

The most burdensome thing that ever happened to me, perhaps, was the day I was playing in the front yard of our East Nashville home with children from the neighborhood.

The game being played was tag. We had to jump over the concrete narrow walkway leading to the porch. If the kid that was "it" kid tagged the one jumping over, either in-flight or if he was on the concrete and got tagged, then he became "it." On this day, I was mastering the complete jump over without touching the walkway, and twisted my left leg and took a hard fall on the edge of the walk. I remember severe leg pain. My father was home, picked me up and carried me into the house. My mother administered the usual treatment for skinned knees and told me to stay off of it. Days passed and my leg was still sore; my left kneecap wasn't as reliable as before.

We moved back to North Nashville shortly after I began the first grade. Our stay in East Nashville was perhaps a year. My mother preferred the old neighborhood.

In East Nashville conditions were the same for my brother, Roy. He was called "Nuttin" because they, too, did not understand his condition.

Anyone who lived in North Nashville was referred to as living in Kalb Hollow. For many years, I thought they were saying Cab Hollow, until someone remarked it was so named because so many people moved there before and during the Depression years from DeKalb County in Tennessee. Others preferred to call it Germantown, because of the presence of so many German families in the area. Back in this different section of North Nashville, we now lived on Madison Street and Roy was called "Curly" because of his naturally curly hair.

School began for me in 1934 in East Nashville. There I began the first grade at Glenn, but transferred to Elliott after only a few weeks, as my mother insisted on returning to North Nashville to live.

CHAPTER 3

Elliott school had the word "Boys" engraved over the door on the Madison Street entrance through which only boys could enter to begin school daily, and "Girls" over the Jefferson Street entrance, at which we girls lined up each morning to enter. I remember we passed by the water fountain which had several spouts, then marched into the restrooms before we could go upstairs to our classroom for the day.

School was fun to me. I liked the stories we read, and my teachers were kind. Our principal, Miss Parham, was a commanding figure over us. No nonsense. I joined Girl Scouts, the first troop at that school. The leader, also my teacher at one point, took advantage of my drawing skills and had me to depict different scenes in chalk of the fun things we scouts did. This was kept on the board, since we met in the same classroom each Friday after school.

My left knee became more and more troublesome. I would go home crying after school, having fallen several times while running or walking on the edge of the sidewalk or playing ball on the graveled yard at recess. I could either amuse or horrify my fellow classmates by straightening the left leg to show how to throw the knee-cap out of place. It was an inconvenience, however, when it moved on its own and I would fall.

There was no money for doctors in those days. A trip to the local pharmacist we called "Doc" was the usual diagnosis and prescription we received. Unless you saw lots of blood or broke a bone, you did not see a doctor, at least not in my family, nor most others. Most babies were delivered at home by the local general practitioner or by a resident or intern from Vanderbilt, as I remember.

Papa worked at the Bridge Company. Mama packed his lunch in a black metal box with rounded top. His thermos was filled with coffee. I don't remember what else went into the lunch box except the fried apple or peach pies she made from dried fruits. When the winter days got bad, the streetcars didn't always run on time. Papa was not daunted, he struck out walking, being sure to arrive at work on time. He was proud of and devoted to his work, being sure that it was done well.

Many Sundays, he, my mother, and I would visit his workplace, an open shed with no shelter from the cold winds blowing over the Cumberland River. A pot-bellied stove was in the center of the shed, used for his blacksmith work. I would jump over the rusty beams of steel, or watch barges on the Cumberland.

It was said in the family that he perfected a machine that was patented over there and that he did the threading for the steel that went into Nashville's tallest church steeple and into the Cordell Hull (Roosevelt's Secretary of State) building; Hull was well known also as a Tennessee statesman.

While my brother, Buster, was still at home, unmarried, I would hear him sing and play the guitar and mandolin with his friends. As a result, I got interested and nagged him into teaching me to play. I managed the guitar, but did not do too well with the mandolin; the strings seemed to cut into my fingers too keenly.

I would entertain the neighborhood kids and join in with those who could also play, though there were few. One night a week during the summertime, a huge projection truck would bring a screen and movie to Morgan Park. On the other nights they would be at Elizabeth Park and other parks in Nashville to give the kids a free movie, sponsored by the Parks Department. There were few benches available, so we sat on the ground (grass was scarce), and used newspapers to sit on.

Many nights when the crowd arrived early and got restless, someone would find a guitar and hoist me into the film truck to sing over the microphone until it got dark enough to show the movie.

All the kids loved Morgan Park. There was a tennis court, swings, monkey bars, seesaws, a ball diamond across from the park, and a wonderful swimming pool, but no diving board. Girls swam for an hour each weekday, as I recall, and the boys were allowed to enter the pool after the girls left. We had a gray-haired policeman, Mr. Bowman, and a park attendant, Mrs. Phillips, who handed out balls, bats, playground equipment for us to use for the day. Additionally, they monitored our behavior. Many of us came early, sat watching and waiting for the two of them to arrive. Mr. Bowman strolled the park and kept "the peace." Just a word from either of them was the law of the park.

Sulphur water from faucets on a small concrete plaza was, for many, the main attraction to the park. Citizens from all over Nashville came with jugs for the water.

In reflecting over one of the unusual memories of the past, I remember a blind man had a tiny building at the Park's entrance. From that he sold candy, gum, popcorn, colas and such. In retrospect, I wonder how he was able to find the merchandise and be sure the change was correct; I cannot remember a single incident suggesting otherwise.

There was also Centenary Methodist Institute (CMI). A free clinic was available. Another area was for clubs, scouts, basketball, baseball teams and boxing. The doors seemed to be open from early morning to evening, depending on the weekday.

On the weekends it was called Teen Town. On Friday and Saturday nights, there were dances for all teens, with either jukebox or a small live band. The latter was a real treat, so it was for special times only. There never was a charge of any kind that I remember.

The State theater opened in North Nashville on 8th and Monroe. We kids would line up for the action films, especially the Cowboy shows on Saturday afternoon.

Mama would let me go alone on Saturday afternoon, because I would be home before dark, even on a winter's day; however, if it was a night movie, I had to go and sit with my brother, Roy.

One night, I remember a group of boys began to jeer at my brother, much to my chagrin. They promised they would be waiting for him to beat him up when he left the movie. We slipped out before the movie was over, but three of them were waiting for him. "Run, Roy!" I yelled, and jumped on the back of the first boy and hooked my arm around his neck holding on to slow him down. I gave Roy a lead. I took the chance that they would not hit a girl—they didn't, much to my relief. He arrived home safely, with me not too far behind.

Summers were fun, too. We had alleys in those days behind each home. Next to the alley, each house had a dump area where garbage and trash were left for the city employees to shovel into trash trucks once a week. Most homes had wood or brick around the area to keep the contents from blowing away; some just let the trash spill into the alley. As kids, we would go along looking for an empty Carnation milk can. We would place it on the ground and stomp with our heel until the can molded to our shoe. One made lots of noise, but two made a lot more fun noise as we ran about.

Another great time was to gather with the black children on Jefferson Street in the yard behind my house. The area belonged to one of their families. The yard was spacious and allowed us to play baseball until dusk. The same alley allowed me to go by their homes as a shortcut to the grocery, dry cleaners, or to run and wave at the miles of trucks of soldiers on their way to Fort Campbell prior to and during World War II. We could hear the rumbling of the big trucks filled with soldiers as they came across the Jefferson Street Bridge.

This same bridge afforded us a good view of the backwaters that flooded all of the areas on the Cumberland

River in the wintertime. The streets in North Nashville were narrow and usually short. Public transportation was our only way to get around. I can remember only one car owner on our street.

Two interesting things about our area; the streets were named after our presidents, and a Catholic cardinal and his sisters had lived on our street for many years.

As in all lives, some rain must fall. It very well did in mine. And there were storms, too, with the rain.

My brother, Roy, used to come in and go out at will, when he became a teenager. If he was not home at mealtime, my mother would become worried that he had met with foul play. She would often go to the door or pace the floor, most of the time sending me out to ask people I knew when they last saw him. This could take me many blocks from my home, and sometimes I would have to stay home from school and look for him if he did not come in the night before.

He was about 18 years old when an official came to the house and informed my parents that he was a nuisance and must be placed in Clover Bottom, an institution for the mentally handicapped. In those days, he was referred to as mentally retarded. I can recall my parents sending him to school, long before I began the first grade. Roy remained in the first grade for several years as they tried to teach him. He disrupted classes, considering them a form of punishment.

Often, I would be entrusted to carry a note from my teacher to his class or to the principal's office and see him sitting in a corner. Upon seeing me, he would wave, grin broadly and yell out, "Hi, Camay (Clara Mai)," to me. The class would giggle, and I would depart red-faced.

He was placed in Clover Bottom in the Donelson area. Most every Sunday, my parents and I would take a bus to downtown, transfer to the Lebanon Road bus and embark nearest the school. From there we would walk to visit him. This was always heartbreaking for my mother. She seemed to age faster. Sometimes he would run away from the home, and they would phone my neighbor's house to reach my mother because we had no phone. Usually, he would be found at my sister Jennie's house a day later. This was several miles from the home, and apparently he walked all the way. Within an hour or so of his arrival, she would somehow report that he was safe with her. This went on for several years.

Another storm occurred while I was in grade school. My sister, Jennie, was pregnant with her second child. Her husband, Louis, worked at the cement plant. One day he was in a room with four other men. The entrance to the room was by ladder. There was an explosion and the men were trapped. They were badly burned before they could be evacuated.

For several weeks, Louis lay in the hospital. My mother and I kept Gene, my nephew, from early morning until late at night, while Jennie sat by his bedside in the hospital. She was with Louis seven days of the week, never thinking of her own health. She went into labor one day, and when the baby boy was born, he was dead. Jennie asked me to be sure and attend the funeral so that I could describe her baby to her. She was not allowed to leave the hospital for several days, so it was my duty to be able to answer her questions about her baby. This was heartbreaking for us all.

When Louis left the hospital months later, he was missing eyebrows, lashes; his eyelids were distorted, and parts of his ears were missing. His face was badly scarred; and I'm sure so was his body that his clothes covered.

After the accident and getting a small settlement from the cement plant since he could never work at manual labor again, he opened a small fruit stand on Jefferson Street. On my visits to the small building, he would often leave me to mind the store, while he went out for an hour or so. It was only a couple of blocks from my home, most of the people knew me, so fear of being alone was not a factor for me.

Later, he bought a small tavern, slangily called a "pie wagon" or "beer joint." Soldiers and locals frequented the place. Their rented house was adjoining the tavern.

His disposition, understandably, began to change. He would close at night and go out on the town. He wore extremely dark sunglasses since the accident, and was never seen without them. Louis seemed to hide behind them.

He would get violent at times and seemed to take his displeasure out on Jennie. His conduct was puzzling to other members of his family who loved Louis but disapproved of his irrational conduct. One day Jennie phoned me. She was frantic, asking me to hurry and take her to the doctor. On arrival, we took a cab to the doctor. Diagnosis: her nose was broken, in addition to other injuries, mostly bruises. We took a bus back that day.

One Sunday, when Jennie was visiting us, Louis came by intoxicated and, as usual, an argument ensued. He drew a gun on Jennie. I stepped between them and told him he would have to shoot me to get to her. My mother was frantic. At this, he calmed down enough to exit quietly. That was some experience, leaving me shaking.

Many times she would phone me to come and mind Gene while she followed Louis or tried to find him. I was too young to understand all of this except I loved them and didn't want anything bad to happen to Jennie, or my nephew, Gene, nor even to Louis.

Another day, children visiting with Gene were playing with candles without permission and caught the doorway drapes afire. She pulled them down but her arms were burned. She called me to come help her.

My sister, Donie, could never assist. She was always, understandably, busy, too. Her husband, Howard, was called into the Army. Donie lived in cramped quarters, and eked out a living from Howard's Army pay and with only a little help from the family. There were eight children, most being born before he entered the military.

A black lady, Eliza, whom we affectionately called "Aunt Liza" came on Mondays to our house to wash the clothes. This was accomplished by washing the clothes on a wash board in a round galvanized tub and rinsing in a similar tub. Laundry was done on the side porch in the summer, and inside the kitchen in the wintertime. Aunt Liza came on Tuesdays to iron—flat irons heated on the coal stove. Later we were blessed with an electric iron.

In the wintertime, the clothes were hung on clotheslines in the backyard (where they were brought in stiff and our hands became chapped from the cold) or they were hung in the kitchen on clotheslines until they dried. Water was brought in from the side yard where we lived. There was no inside plumbing. It came from a hydrant and filled the buckets for drinking (from a dipper) or for getting a bath in the big galvanized tub. Heat and hot water were provided by the kitchen coal stove. When not in use, the bath tub hung on the fence that led into the backyard.

Home was a rented duplex consisting of four rooms. From the front door you could see into my parents' room to the kitchen and beyond that to the "junk" room. There our clothes hung on hangers on a line (our make-shift closet), the trunk of old photos was kept, the biscuit board hung, and the dirty laundry was kept. Our only heat was from a front room grate (small fireplace).

From the junk room door we could exit, take a right turn and go into the dirt cellar where Mama kept her foods that she canned.

CHAPTER 4

The summer when I was 13, a preacher that had a radio ministry came to town to have an open air revival. He was M. F. Hamm, an elderly man. Rustic wooden benches were hastily put up for use, as well as the podium and platforms from the same materials. Decades later, I learned that he was influential in the life of a teen-aged Billy Graham, who became well known and respected as a minister himself in ensuing years.

Though my parents had been brought up as Methodists, they seldom went to church. I remember going with girl friends of mine to various Sunday schools, but never routinely. An open-air revival or a vacation Bible school often attracted us kids during our summers, however.

I listened intently, as Dr. Hamm walked back and forth on the wooden platform, sometimes pounding the pulpit for emphasis. He certainly was clear in what he said, and it was as though he was speaking right to me, that he could see what was in my life that needed changing. When he stopped preaching and asked for everyone that knew God to turn their backs to him, I could not be truthful if I turned around. It was not as if I had done really bad things, but enough that God was not first in my life as he said God should be.

"Mama, Papa, is it okay if I go down front?" They nodded approval. They had already turned their backs to Dr. Hamm and were facing the rear. Several people were walking down the aisles and going toward the front. I followed. He prayed a prayer of dedication of our lives and forgiveness for our transgressions. That simple, but it changed my life completely. Any act of deliberate wrong of any kind would mean that I did not love God as I should. My parents had enough confidence in me that Mama forked out fifty cents per week for many weeks to buy me a Bible. I knew very little about it, except for Sunday school stories. That summer, I read multiple chapters per day. Many years later, my grandson, Jamian, to please me, read a special chapter in Psalms to fit his problem. He told me by phone, "Granny, I read the modern words, not the Shakespearean one (King James Version)." I laughed because it brought back memories of my being unfamiliar with the Bible, too.

When I returned to school that September, I was determined to study hard, make good grades, because I did not want anyone to say I was a Christian because I was stupid. I wanted to be a leader and make something of my life. This was an ambitious undertaking, a determined one.

In 1940, I entered the seventh grade, the first year our high school in North Nashville opened. There, all six grades for graduation could be completed.

In the ninth grade English class, we were asked to write a paper on any subject we chose. Mine was a stirring treatise on the way black people were treated: having to take the backseat of a bus, use separate restrooms, not be allowed to eat in most restaurants, etc. The paper went on to cover many inequities. Our teacher read it aloud to the class. She was pleased with it and said my thinking was beyond my age. She also discussed it with her husband, who worked in the office of the Bridge Company where my father worked. Papa came home happy that they were so moved by my topic. To me black people hurt and bled just like the rest of us, and the only difference was the pigment of the skin. All of us knew people who brought grief to others, but it had nothing to do with the skin pigment. That year when the class superlatives were chosen, I was voted Most Likely to Succeed.

My mother's health was declining. She was frail and thin. Her asthma was more severe in the wintertime. Summers were also hard on her, because in those days, few people had any cooling system except for a piece of cardboard stapled to a thin handle. This served as a fan.

A small oscillating fan, and finally a refrigerator to replace the icebox came to us in the late l930s. An indoor bath was not to be for me until the early 1950s.

A ceiling fan was a luxury in most churches, and if a business had air-conditioning in later years, it was advertised on the door: "Air-Conditioned Inside."

In the fall, Papa would get a load of wood and, using a portable tree stump, he would chop kindling to start the coal fires we had in the winter, and to stoke the cook stove my mother used all year. The coal was dumped into our shed by the alley, and we stacked wood against one wall.

Before dusk each night, we filled scuttles of coal, and brought wood to our side porch. When the scuttle got empty in our one grate (fireplace) in the front room, we would fetch another full one to replace it. Also, the stove went out after supper, so the only heat was from the fireplace. Many times, we hiked our dresses in the back and put our legs close to the fire for quick warmth when we came in. The grate would go out shortly after we went to bed, so there was no heat until Papa built a fire in the grate in the morning and then another in the kitchen stove for my mother to prepare breakfast. It must've been bitter cold for him, but we were still warm under the several layers of homemade quilts my mother made.

In grade school, my warmth was provided by long underwear with a seat panel that buttoned up, long cotton stockings, and shoes that had to be half-soled (repaired) when a hole wore through from constant wear. A worn pair had to suffice the couple of days it took the shoe shop to put on new soles. Getting a new pair of shoes was a very special occasion. Socks were mended until they were no longer useful.

One of my daily jobs was to get a pan of soapy water and wipe up the ash residue after one of us poked the fire or ran the poker through the openings in the grate to rekindle the fire and make it burn longer. This chore was repeated several times a day.

There were no cabinets in the kitchen, only one handmade rustic "safe" with glass windows that revealed a few good pieces of crystal on the top shelf. The lower shelves held every day plates, cups, saucers, and serving bowls—all mismatched. A drawer under it was for the cutlery, knives, flatware of that day, definitely not silver nor silver-plated. Then below that was storage for pots and pans, enclosed by solid doors. In the corner was a table on which my mother put staples and condiments, canned goods, flour, sugar, and other things for cooking. It was covered by a checked tablecloth. This was our "cook table." The dining table had been made by Papa. It was covered by an oilcloth that could be wiped, and replaced when all the design had been worn away.

Our sewing machine was an old pedal Singer. My mother made many linings and sewed many squares for quilts on that machine. A favorite from it for me was the bonnet she would make to match hers each summer. This was to shield us when we went outside to hang clothes on the line to dry. They hung on the aforementioned line strung across the length of the kitchen during the winter months, the clothes that would otherwise come in "stiff as a board" (her description of frozen clothes).

Canned goods she made went into our dirt cellar. When she made grape jelly she would put the cooked grapes into a cloth bag and let me squeeze as she held the bag. The liquid from the bag's squeezed contents became the jelly. Needless to say, my hands and nails were purple for a few days.

She never spared the rod. My father hit me only once that I remember, never spanked me, but a sound thrashing from the belt Mama kept handy was punishment if I was late coming home or going someplace she disapproved. The summer that Dr. Hamm preached changed that, too. Being more responsible for my conduct seemed important and the sensible thing to do.

My mother's health seemed to grow worse every winter. She had asthma, high blood pressure, and her lungs were weakened by having had pneumonia twice. Mama never was overweight in her life; she weighed less than 100 pounds. She never cut her hair in her lifetime and wore her gray hair in a bun atop her head. Because of ill health, many of her teeth were missing.

Often, when she was ill, I would sit her up in the bed and hold her there as I persuaded her to eat. Papa seemed to get quieter, more pensive. My brother, Mac, saw him on the bridge one day as he drove to his home from work.

"Clara, Papa was looking down at the water as if he planned to jump. I turned around at the corner of the bridge and went back to get him into the car and he let me drive him home. Keep an eye on him!" He and my sister-in-law, Rose, seemed to come more often after that. I noticed, also, that Papa began to go uptown on Saturday morning more frequently. He would come home with a bottle and drink off and on until time to go to work on Monday morning.

Times were difficult for me. I plunged into my schoolwork. It was so good to go to a warm school, join the band, go to the teen dances, and try for every honor that I could get. My long-range ambition was to be a doctor, to get out of my current standard of living, and to make a good future for my family and me. Visions of a beautiful home and mixing with intelligent people began to cloud my mind.

During this time, I took piano lessons from a teacher that only charged me fifty cents per hour. This was a lot of money to my family, but it added to my musical knowledge. About that time, a friend who played the French horn in the school band asked me to join and learn the flute. They needed a flute player. Later, I was elected president of the band. I took so many classes to get credits there was no time for lunch; so I ate hurriedly between classes. College tuition was out of the question, so, perhaps someone would notice my diverse achievements and give me a "break"...somehow.

There were constant reminders that these were still Post-Depression days. When visiting some school friends, I noticed their mattresses were sometimes not covered by sheets, completely bare, and there was no linoleum on the floor. Most certainly, few had an area carpet on the floor. If so, the carpets were hung on the line and beaten, as no one had an electric vacuum cleaner.

Furniture was scarce for us. We hung our coats and sweaters behind the door on nails. The other clothes went into bureau drawers or hung in the junk room.

My request for a desk was granted by my father. He went to town on one Saturday morning, and that afternoon, it was delivered along with a lamp (the only one in the house, since light bulbs hung down from the ceiling in the center of each room for lighting) and a desk chair. Later, he allowed me to buy some bronze and marble book ends. The desk was in the corner by the front door. So I often had to go to the grate and warm my hands, because that corner of the room got very little heat from the small fireplace.

Our next-door neighbors were an elderly father, a mother and daughter (who never married). They had all the amenities for which I wished: inside bathroom, sink in the kitchen, gas lights on the walls, a push lawnmower, a fenced flower garden, an automobile and a large backyard with an enclosed garage. Note: We cut our grass with scissors. Needless to say, our front yard was very small.

When my neighbor had guests, many times they would call me over to meet them. There was a bare spot in their hedge for me to shortcut through. They were German and enjoyed some of the most prominent people in Nashville in that day. They were related to many of them, too. A fun thing for me was to visit them and look at pictures through the kaleidoscope which appeared to be 3D. Or I would quietly climb on the horizontal bottom two by four of our fence and observe the guests touring their small garden. It was always full of flowers.

My parents were visiting a cousin, Alice, on the Sunday that Pearl Harbor was attacked. The radio kept talking about it; my knowledge of what this meant was nil. They hurried home so that they could stay close to the radio for more word.

As soon as they reached our door, I met them with the question, "What does this mean, Papa?"

"It means we are at war." He looked sad and nervous. Shortly, we heard the yelling of the newspaper boy as he came up the street, "Extra. Extra. Read all about it! Japanese attack Pearl Harbor. WAR." He drew all our neighbors to the street to buy his papers. Eventually, Buster was drafted into the Army. Prior to his draft, he was trained in Dayton, Ohio to teach instrument flying.

His expertise was not used. He was put in the infantry instead and also repaired watches.

Papa's employer began to build mine sweepers for the Navy. Therefore, Papa had to work longer hours to keep up orders, especially pertaining to war supplies.

Before his draft, Buster got me actively going to the Presbyterian Church he attended with wife, Dorothy. She was the Church pianist and organist, at times when the pastor's wife did not play. Many times they did duets, playing both piano and organ. They learned that I could sing and, later, I joined the choir, doing soprano solos, and took the tenor or alto parts when needed in a trio or if a section was lacking in volume.

If I performed at a wedding, usually other performances followed in private homes, churches or wherever. During the war, one interesting occasion was to solo on the stage of the War Memorial Auditorium in downtown Nashville, with our Girls Cadet Corps singing with me. My parents were there to hear me—quite a different performance than the Carnival "display" in my tender years. In the Cadet Corps, there were seven officers. I was a lieutenant and the chaplain.

Nashville's chief of police for almost twenty years was a classmate of mine from the seventh grade. When nominations for President of the Student Body were given, he nominated me. I was the first Junior and the first girl to run for the office. Appreciatively, I captured an overwhelming majority of the votes. It was important to me to keep every promise made during the campaign, and I fulfilled that.

Gratefully, there were other accomplishments: the Honor Roll, participating in band concerts and parades, my Senior year becoming co-editor of the North Star newspaper, President of the marching and concert bands, President of the Student Government, Most Likely to Succeed, Daughters of the American Revolution medalist, Civitan medalist and Civitan essay winner, and reelected President of the Student Body.

At the same time, I had been teaching a Junior class of boys at church. When asked at age 16, the Church felt my understanding of the Bible was sufficient for the responsibility. This was a privilege to be a teacher. The boys proved to be respectful and anxious to learn.

President Roosevelt died during my time in office. The School's principal asked me to help present our tribute to him. It was a solemn event.

About this time, my mother had several strokes, with the last being most severe. Buster was in Europe in the Army. Dorothy and I went to the Red Cross with the word from her doctor that Mama was dying, and Buster was needed at home.

CHAPTER 5

Many days my school attendance was limited to one hour (going to turn in my homework and getting new assignments). Mama could not be left alone and no help could be found. My sisters had their small children, and domestic help was unavailable at the price we could pay. They did come for an hour or two here and there. A maidenly lady (Miss Mary) who passed my house every day, with her brother (Mr. Will) on the way to mass would sometimes sit with Mama. Both were always clad in black; she, in long dress and high top shoes, he, in suit and tie. They were devout and loving people.

One of my most respected teachers stopped me in the hall one day, then began to walk with me. It was an honor to walk with a teacher, most especially this one.

Mrs. Jackson said, "I had no idea you had been carrying such personal loads all these years. Surely God gave you your intelligence plus the part your brother did not get. Mr. Noel (our principal) has finally told us about this; he has kept your secrets a long time."

I shall never forget this tribute from so fine a lady. She was elderly and taught (of all subjects) Civics. Indeed, something to remember always.

Many times, my father asked me to quit high school and stay home with Mama, since the cost of keeping me in school was so high, and there was no one to be with her all the time. This was when I asked if I could go just part-time to get my lessons and turn in the ones I had finished.

Mama apparently had several small strokes, and her disposition worsened, too.

Jennie and Louis divorced. My presence was needed at the divorce trial (the first trial ever for me to observe). Jennie wanted me there for support; she cried during the whole heartbreaking court action. Before his accident, my prediction was that their marriage would always endure and be a happy one. Now it was over.

The marriage was gone, but Louis continued to go to the house causing disturbances inside and outside. The neighbors feared for Jennie's life and would call the police. On one such occasion, they arrested him. He resisted and fought with them down the front porch stairs and had to be forcefully pushed inside the police car, so Jennie said.

The story was that he had some injuries and the police took him to General Hospital, where the police said they were caused by his falls.

Witnesses said that Louis replied with several oaths, "No. You kept beating me with that club." He lived only a few days after that.

Since school and my church provided me such a happy "outlet," boys were out of the question; there was no time for such frivolity. However, that was to change.

While walking home from school with a friend she observed a boyfriend going into a building and emerging from the other end. She called out to him; he caught up with us.

"Red, this is my friend, Clara."

"Yeah, I know her from school." He smiled at me.

Knowing she liked him from her chatter about this redhead, my first thought was to get them together more often. There was a church gathering for young people going on, and she came to our church often.

"How about coming to the church on the corner tonight with Velma?"

"Will you be there?" He asked quickly.

Thinking nothing of the question, my answer was affirmative.

He left us after a few more words, except to ask me where I lived. Soon, she turned down 8th Avenue, promising to see me later.

Upon reaching home, getting my coat off and telling Mama what transpired for the day, there was a knock at the door. There Red stood with his bag of papers slung across his shoulder and our newspaper in his hand.

"Hello again. I deliver papers every morning and evening, and I swapped routes with Herbert today so that I could bring yours to you. Will I see you later tonight?"

I was stunned, muttering yes and hurrying to get the door closed.

Sure enough, there he was at church. Velma was not there.

He followed me out of the church after the service and walked me home. I suggested that Velma might not like him walking me home. He was not to be deterred, saying that they both dated other people and saw each other occasionally. That was not the opinion she gave to me in our brief conversation about him.

Red was several inches taller than I, muscular from boxing, playing football and basketball. He was quite handsome, though he did have red hair. (Not my favorite color for hair.).

He was well known all over Nashville for his athletic abilities, I soon learned. A favorite of the sports editor of the morning newspaper, he was often written up in the sports section for his boxing expertise and victories. Boxing was a sport that seemed barbaric to me, but he spoke of it with admiration.

Every time I turned around, he seemed to be there, constantly wanting to see me.

Finally, I relented and dates followed.

When we walked on Church Street (one of Nashville's busiest), half the people spoke to him. Some yelled from across the street. It seemed everywhere we turned people knew him and liked him. From his paper routes, he had money, so we got to go to town on Saturday night, see a movie or bowl, and then go to a favorite place to eat.

We spoke about many things. He boasted that if there was a speeding ticket in one of his friend's cars, or he happened to be in the wrong place and some of his buddies started a fight on purpose just to watch him finish it for them, and they were arrested and fined, he would be called to come get his fine money back. Red seemed to know the "right" people.

Since he was from a broken alcoholic home, he had to start at a young age to selling newspapers on the streets at night to provide for himself. There was no other way; he was homeless unless one of his friends invited him home to spend the night with them. Going to school was erratic for him. Apparently, he went only to play sports. The more I learned, the more I felt sad for his past and future. He delivered papers in all kinds of weather with minimum appropriate clothes on. Was it because he was not taught to dress warmly in the winter months, or could he not afford such since he had to pay for his existence?

Red learned to direct soldiers on the streets from Fort Campbell and other war facilities to liquor outlets or even to get the liquor for them. He also knew where to find the girls for them. Since I was a "nice" girl, he only hinted about how he earned his money. He was definitely "street smart." There was always good money in tips for him.

He could not do enough to please me, it seemed; he said he had not met a girl like me before.

Since he had no car, our dates, winter and summer, were usually long strolls on the dim streets with a stop at a café or a drugstore ice cream counter. Sometimes, it was a long walk after his football or basketball game. He tried to see me as often as he was allowed by me. He was comfortable to be with, and certainly a break from my duties at home. His presence seemed an escape, diversion.

We dated several times before he asked to kiss me. This was a first for me, so I kept putting him off. One night on one of the darkened streets, he suddenly spun me around, pulled me close to him and kissed me. His arms were strong and demanding; I had no time to object. It was exciting; feelings I had never had before for anyone. My head was in a swirl. It was wonderful.

But what would my mother and father think about me? What was happening? His lips came down on mine the second time, and I pushed him away. He apologized for not asking.

"I've been wanting to kiss you for a long time and couldn't wait any longer," he whispered.

My parents had never been impressed when I would come home and tell them of earning a new award, election or citation, especially being a female. Since neither had gone past the sixth grade, high school or upper education was not familiar to them. True, with their many accomplishments (my father had earned a patent for his company on a machine and had worked extremely hard for his family; Mama's knowledge came from hard times and observations), my experiences paled in comparison. When I would come home with a new honor, they would respond with a "that's nice" (ho-hum) attitude. Their kid could not possibly be outstanding, and a new citation was just one among many similar awards given to the "average" student. Nothing special.

Then one day a man came to speak to our student body. Information came to me from the principal about him. In walking down the hall and onto the stage with him to introduce him, he mentioned the Bridge Company as his next place to speak, to all the war effort employees. I told him my father worked there. He asked, "Is your father, Shorty Emery?" And then he quoted to me the number of years my father had worked there. The speaker was from New York.

At the Bridge Company that afternoon, all the employees were seated around the platform from which he spoke.

He mentioned having been to North High, told of me and my accomplishments and asked my father to stand up and be recognized. Papa could not hear very well and thought the men around him were razzing him, and this was a bad joke. The owner of the company came down, took him by the arm and personally escorted him to the platform to sit. Papa was stunned by the attention given him.

The magazine of the Alabama and Nashville companies did a feature story on me, the first student to be recognized by the publication.

That evening Papa said, "Kid, why didn't you ever tell me about all you have been doing?"

I replied, "I did, Papa but you never seemed interested."

Later, he came home and proudly related the teasing from his fellow workers asking where I got my intelligence. Also, the editor of the publication said he was swamped with requests by other employees to print stories about their children. Papa chuckled at this.

World War II was coming to a close. Buster was finally shipped home.

Mama had a severe stroke, but she pulled through. The paralysis affected one eye, as well as other parts of her small body. The eye seemed to remain in one place as the other one moved to follow an object. She eventually walked but dragged one foot; the hand on that side was limp and would not respond. She talked with a slur and was not intelligible many times;. her manner was that of a small child.

Improvement allowed her to attend my graduation. She, Papa, and other members of the family saw me graduate. My vocal solo was "The Lord's Prayer." At this time, the Daughters of the American Revolution Medal and the Civitan Medal were given to me. My graduation made me sad, because it meant no longer seeing all the friends so dear to me.

After graduation, I had a job within five days. Papa soon informed me that Mama would have to go to a nursing home, since care for her was not practical at home. She also had additional health problems.

He seemed like a very old man now; he looked beaten, downtrodden; not the same; his spirit was gone.

There was little conversation at home; the house seemed quiet all the time.

The rare times that I agreed to see Red were fun, a diversion, an escape from so many daily decisions that came from problems that went around and around and never seemed to have solutions.

Mama went into the nursing home across from the State Theater where my brother and I had gone to Saturday matinée cowboy shows.

Papa would come home after work and, while I prepared the evening meal, he would go to visit with her.

One late evening after a visit with Mama, I left the nursing home to go home and prepare the meal for Papa and me. Her breathing had been so laborious, it could be heard from the first-floor stairway that led to the hall adjoining her room.

Later at home, as I finished preparing the meal, my brother, Mac, quietly came in the side door. One look at his face told me she was gone.

He sobbed, "Mama died a few minutes ago." We sat for a few minutes and said little but cried openly. Soon he left to go get my father to bring him home for the night. Lavelle, a church friend of mine, was at her side, too, at the end.

We drove to Dover and buried her in the graveyard next to Fort Donelson, a Civil War battle ground. All around were headstones of relatives (those not resting in plots on the family farms grounds).

My grief was deep, felt in many ways. I can remember standing by the window during the first rain after the burial. The day was bitter cold and I was thinking about my mother lying in a cold ground, while I was inside the warm house.

Red and I began to see each other more often. He would not take no for an answer when he said he was going to see me. He went another year to high school to play football and to box. He won several titles in boxing, and went to New York as a reward for one of them. Spending money for the trip was given to him in gifts from the pie wagon (diner) customers where he worked sometimes. Another contributor was Henry, the husband of Minnie Pearl, the country star comedienne, who was a boxing fan and friend of Red's. He and Minnie often stopped at the eating place for the tasty stew on their way to the airport outside North Nashville. Henry's plane was housed at this airport.

My doubts that the marriage he proposed would fail began to grow. However, he would passionately kiss me, swear that he would be a wonderful, devoted husband, that he needed a chance to have a good home he had never had before. I determined to stop his visits, but he begged and swore his life on his love for me. He would set the date for our marriage, and when the time came close, I would back out. He vowed that I could go to school after we were married, but for now to please give him a happy home.

Surely this eagerness on his part to be married was the most sincere display of love that any person could show, so how could I question his sincerity?

How naïve and gullible I was. Later, I would ask myself how anyone who professed to have half a brain could be so stupid as I was to have believed all this.

We eloped two years after I graduated. We kept it a secret for about two months. I was afraid this news would adversely affect my father's health.

Several months before, I had sung for the formal wedding of the couple that took us to be married. Max and Mattie Lou were trusted friends and they, also, seemed to share my faith in him. Mattie Lou had graduated with me.

Most of the weddings for which I sang were in homes or churches. There, the family of a future bride or groom would hear me sing at a wedding and ask me to solo for their upcoming event. One month there were five weddings, for which I sang. It was such a pleasure to participate.

Our marriage took place about four months before my mother's passing.

"Papa, please sit down; I have something to tell you," I said, one evening after we finished supper (lunch was dinner in those days, and dinner was supper to us).

"This is difficult for me to tell you… Red and I married in July, and we want to be together."

He did not reply for what seemed a long time, just looked at the wall, not at me, with an ashen face, drained of color. He looked defeated and sad, as if about to faint or cry.

"It would not work out for me to stay here with you two, so I will find me a place that has room and board and will move out," he said, barely audible.

The next weekend he took his clothes, what few there were, and moved to the west part of Nashville, boarding on West End Avenue. He planned to take his meals elsewhere. The place he chose to go was only a couple of houses away. The proprietor was an interesting lady. She had sold her farm after her husband's death. He had died young and she was left on the farm with two small daughters to rear alone.

She moved to Nashville and became a fraternity house mother. Being an excellent cook with an impeccable reputation earned her this job to support her daughters and herself.

She told me how she had to mother the young men, often with rules and then check on their response to her instructions.

"I'm coming upstairs now. Are you all dressed? I have to check a room" for whatever reason she had. She was doing a wonderful job, pleasing the men of the fraternity and the University.

After some time as house mother, she decided she would be happier having boarders as her daughters, Della and Adelia, were getting older.

Subsequently, she bought a house on West End and took in boarders; also cooked for outsiders who had sleeping quarters elsewhere but wanted home-cooked meals. My father was among them.

After several months, their friendship ripened. This was pleasing for me to hear, because it had been so many years since he laughed so easily.

In the meantime, I visited the neighborhood furniture store, and chose some new furniture. Our landlady's nephew agreed to paper our side of the duplex if I furnished the paper. I painted the woodwork, the old table and chairs and the "safe" (floor cabinet). I had wall-to-wall carpeting installed; a sink was put into the kitchen; blinds and drapes were put up. When I finished, it did not look like the same place.

Making sure that I was the perfect (working) housewife, I had cotton tablecloths instead of oilcloths on the table, cloth napkins for evening meals. I hurried to get the house cleaned before going to work and rushed home to get the evening meals ready.

Everything was "honeymoonish" for a few months, then Red began to come home at erratic hours. He was seldom on time for dinner nor dependable to keep his word on where he was going or when he would be back.

He liked to sell produce. This was disrupting, because he wanted to have his own wagon with it being horse drawn, selling the produce street by selected street.

We had an oil heater put in the bedroom; it heated the living room and kitchen, too. There was no need for the coal house, so he put the horse in there where it could be stabled and fed.

The spring and summer allowed vegetables for him to sell, peddle on the streets, but wintertime meant no work for him. He would take a job in the winter, but would give it up for the peddling when spring rolled around.

This was not dependable, so we would argue. His present job course offered no future. This problem was never envisioned by me, since I assumed that everyone chose a steady job.

A reality hit me one day in a conversation with Red. He could not read or write past the (approximately) second grade level. Why had this not been realized by me before? Then my mind went back to the clues that were not recognized by me. Other girls wrote notes to me in school for him; he never wrote me if he took a trip during school years. His high school subjects were well selected. The teachers apparently were asked by the principal to promote him even though he did not deserve to be—only because he excelled in sports.

He never read a menu in a restaurant, but would order familiar items. On and on my mind tumbled with this dismaying revelation. I was repulsed, but knew it could be overcome. I could teach him to read. I approached him with this knowledge, told him my solution, but he refused to learn, saying reading gave him headaches. Apparently it was self-discipline that was lacking. The future looked so bleak, but as an old saying went: I had made my bed and had to lie in it. In other words, I had to make the best of the situation.

There were many friends for us both. Many came to share a meal with us, go on a picnic, eat out, go to a baseball game (Sulphur Dell was within five city blocks), or go watch him box until he finally gave it up shortly after our marriage.

His erratic behavior and irresponsibility began to surface even more. He sometimes acted like a single man with no responsibilities. It was as though he could not grow up and wanted to remain a teenager.

When confronted with, "Red, we need to pay the rent and the furniture bills." His usual reply was, "Let them worry about me for a change. I have worried about them long enough." Then another argument would ensue. I tried everything: to be a wife, a lover, a friend, any role I could conceive to remind him that we had taken vows to honor each other in sickness or in health. What was wrong? Nothing worked, except at sporadic times.

He got a city job at the airport. Finally, it seemed that all would be well. He worked replacing lights on the runways and other jobs relating to the airport.

One night he phoned that his car had broken down on Jefferson Street, which was on our side of town. I waited supper for him for a couple of hours with no call from him as to how the repairs were coming along. I suspected he had lied, so I took the bus at the corner, transferred uptown to the Murfreesboro Road bus to go toward the airport. It was by then about 9 p.m. I got off the bus near the airport, remembering a beer joint I had seen on one of our Sunday rides in that direction. Sure enough, his car was in the parking lot.

He soon came outside and passed our car on his way to the outside men's restroom. It was unlocked and my windows were down. When he passed by the car, I leaned out the window. "When did Jefferson Street turn into Murfreesboro Road?" I asked to his complete surprise and shock.

"I'll go in and finish the shuffleboard game and be right out," he replied.

Within the hour he angrily got in the car, slamming his door, speedily exiting the parking lot saying, "I'm over 21, and I will do as I please." Certainly, a far cry from the promises he made to me before marriage.

What had I gotten myself into? How could my desire to believe him overcome my good sense reasoning? Or was good sense reasoning even a part of my makeup? He was charming to a fault, good-looking, rugged, all the physical attributes a woman could want. That was it. Had my chaste years left me with the inability to choose a proper husband and lover? Oh well, it was too late now to figure it out.

Billy and Margaret were good friends of Red's. He invited them over. We four began to go out together. The usual was for Margaret and me to sit in the car on weekend nights and chat while the two husbands shot pool. This soon got monotonous, but it beat sitting at home waiting for them. At least we could chat with a passing friend or two, if they happened by.

One Sunday afternoon, they came over. During the preparation of the tasty meal I planned, Red said that he and Billy would go shoot a little pool, but would be back in plenty of time because they were hungry.

Time passed. The meal was ready to be served. No Red and no Billy.

"Where could they be, Margaret?"

"You know them. We can expect them when we see them coming," she replied cynically. We waited yet another hour.

"Do you suppose they had a wreck?" She frowned as she asked.

I replied, "Surely they would have phoned us if they ran into trouble of some kind. I know, let's go in your car and look for them! They should be somewhere in this part of town. I have an extra car key that I keep in the bookcase. I bet Red has forgotten that I still have it. If they are still playing with complete disregard for us waiting for them, I'd like to teach them a good lesson for a change. We can use the spare key to take Red's car."

We locked the door and hurried away, heading toward the many joints we knew they frequented.

After much crisscrossing of the streets we thought them to be, and after scanning the neighborhoods for Red's car, we found it on Buchanan Street. We parked opposite the saloon and down the street to make sure they could not see us if they came out. Then I revealed to Margaret my plot.

"Let's park a block around the corner on 11th Avenue, in the alley. Red's car is not right in front of the tavern, so they can't see you take it. Then you can walk over there, get into his car and drive it around close to us here and park it! When they finally come out, they will think somebody has stolen it. We'll hurry home and wait for the phone to ring. We have to be fast." We giggled with excitement.

"They have complete disregard for us, not caring that dinner has been waiting hours for them," Margaret said, as we drove into an alley and parked.

I waited in her car while she went for Red's car. She positioned it on the street so that it could not be easily seen. I joined her in his car for a moment while we burst out in laughter. Then we hastily went back into the alley and drove away in her car.

We hurried home and rushed into the house. Sure enough, within minutes the phone rang and it was Red. He was near hysteria, "Clara, somebody has stolen my car."

"Where are you?" I sympathetically replied.

"Here on Buchanan Street. Billy and I stopped and got a beer and lost count of the time. I've called the police; they're on the way to get my information," he said with panic in his voice.

"Margaret, and I'll drive out to get you and Billy so that we can drive around to help you try to find it. This may be futile, because they are probably already out of town by now. Why didn't you come home earlier like you promised and this would have never happened?"

"I'm sorry, honey. I won't do this again. What am I going to do without a car?"

"Ride the bus like I do, I guess," I quipped.

We drove out to pick them up, laughing at the dilemma. Needless to say, we took our time getting there.

We picked Red and Billy up and started driving in circles as Red instructed, being careful to avoid THE street. When we returned to the tavern, the police said the car was parked nearby. They had found it.

Driving home, we asked questions of Red. He was clearly shaken and happy to be driving his car. It was undamaged, of course. Billy drove his own car to my house.

"Where did they find it?" Margaret asked.

"On 11th Avenue. We didn't go up that street. Remember? Some old people sitting on their porch told the cops that two women got out of it," he said in disbelief.

"Two women?" I snapped.

"Honey, I have no idea who they were," he said with shaking voice.

"Sounds like you two let two familiar women drive your car. How else would they have the keys?" I asked.

"I swear there were no women in the place today," his voice quivered.

To this I got silent and stayed that way until we reached home. It was a quiet meal, and Billy and Margaret left early.

This event made him a remarkably good husband for about two weeks; then the usual, non-acceptable conduct began again. Where was our marriage going? What future did we have together?

Soon, Papa announced that he was marrying the lady where he took his meals. After meeting her, I knew she would be exceptionally good for him. They married shortly thereafter.

"What would you like me to call you?" I asked when they visited me.

"What would you like to call me? Whatever you wish," she smiled.

"Would Mother Nola be all right with you?" I asked. It had to be respectful and affectionate, because I had the highest regard for her and knew I would grow to love her. My prediction would come true.

CHAPTER 6

"Is that what is wrong with me?" I asked the doctor one spring afternoon following an examination.

"No. That is what is RIGHT with you," he smiled as he told me I was pregnant. My suspicions were confirmed.

Coming out of his office in a daze, I said aloud to myself, "What have I done?"

This seemed to cement the misery of my marriage. A child was coming. How could I exit the marriage now?

Easter came. On the day before, Red presented me with two gifts. A corsage of miniature roses (useless, because we were not going anywhere for me to wear it and would, therefore, die in the refrigerator) and the other was a live rabbit. I really tried not to show my dismay with these inappropriate gifts.

Within days, the flowers died, but the rabbit remained. It was small, so I put it in a shoe box at night so that it would not roam the house. I weighed the shoe box lid down with books, after punching holes in the side of the box so that the rabbit could get air. But, the books weren't heavy enough, and. the next morning, I found the rabbit had escaped, roamed the house all night, chewing things at will. To my disgust, it had eaten the edges of my rubber sole shoes. What to do with this indoor monster?

Within a few hours, it became the pet of my small nephew. Jimmy was delighted. However, the rabbit wore out its welcome. It was relegated to only the bathroom. A few days later, I phoned and he had been given to another family. Relieved, I did not ask the name of that family.

We were in our third year of marriage when Teresa was born. After her birth, I drew six weeks of unemployment compensation. Then the bank hired me. When Teresa was about one year old, the University of Tennessee began to offer classes. They were limited and offered only in the evenings, as I recall.

On seeing the available classes, public speaking was a course that could be a starter for me and would require very little outside work and study. Red agreed to watch Teresa the one night each week for me to go to class. This seemed a good beginning to get credits. It was a slow beginning, but it was a beginning

Classes were held in different locations about town, as there was no University of Tennessee Building. This was also a trial to see if the demand was there. My class was to be held at the old high school downtown.

Extemporaneous speaking was a snap for me, because of my background as student body president those two years and being in high school plays. So, I anticipated no problems. The class was enjoyable. One evening, the professor announced that we were going to be learning to properly introduce ourselves and others in a formal situation. The lady sitting next to me, with whom I often chatted before class, told me the professor had an excellent background, with the experience of directing some of television's earliest shows. She was a script writer for a local radio station.

On announcing the "project," he said that we would be combining with the other class on a social basis at his home. I was elected as spokesperson from our class to plan the event. He announced that we representatives would be meeting at his home later in the week to finalize the plans together. As instructed, I arrived and patiently waited on the front steps of the school for his class to end on the appointed evening. To my surprise, no one came out with him.

"The other class members cannot make it tonight, so we will go on," he said to a surprised me.

It was now about eight o'clock in the evening. I hoped that his home was near, so that we could get the preparations over and I could get home soon. Instead, we headed out Clarksville Highway. Our conversation on the way was polite, but I felt uncomfortable.

Why should I feel restless about this situation? This was an important, well-respected teacher and professor. In addition, and most importantly, he probably had a wife and children awaiting our arrival. This was conceited of me to imagine the man would give me a second glance. How could my imagination be so distorted and suspicious, certainly not in this case?

When we left the highway, we began to ride up a hill. On arrival at the house at the top, there was only an outside light on. Any moment I expected his wife to drive up, a lovely educated companion.

We went inside; he took my coat. Then he offered me a beverage; I drank water. Shortly, after turning on all the lights, he began to take me on a tour of the house. My thoughts were of appreciation that my presence was welcome, but I had to hurry through this and get home.

Every time my conversation would go toward the object of my visit, he would show me souvenirs of his war years as a Major in the military: swords, medals and other items that interested him. By that time I was getting restless, and my heart began to beat fast. I was quite uneasy. It was obvious that I was brought there under false pretenses, and I was too naïve to see it.

"Would you please take me home? My husband will be very worried about me."

I could feel myself shaking inside, also very angry with myself for falling into this situation, for being so stupid.

To ease my embarrassment, I said that we could have this another night when the others would be present from the other class. Actually, I resolved never to return to his class, but did not indicate that to him. Upon going outside to get in the car, my teeth began to chatter and I began to shake from the cold night air and the humility I felt.

On the way home, he touched me only once and that was to hold my hand briefly and say, "I shall never forget you. If there is anything you ever want, you know where to find me. You have indicated that you want an education; I will pay for it if you will see me."

By now, it was nearly ten p.m. When we reached the front of my house, Red stormed out of the door. Apparently he was watching for me.

I lowered my window about three inches, "Hi, honey. I'm sorry to be so late, the others had to be dropped off first."

This was a lie, but I feared for my life, as well as the professor's. Red reached through the small space, grabbed my hair and tried to pull me through the glass window. I screamed and pulled back. He let go and began to run around the rear of the car to the professor's side.

"I'm going to kill you," Red yelled over and over.

The professor's window was rolled down, and he hastily tried to remedy this before Red could get to his door. But Red was quick, reached inside and grabbed him by the front of his trench coat and tried to pull him through the window. The professor clung to the steering wheel and, as he did, he inadvertently turned the right front wheels toward the curb and fence.

Red could not get him through the small space because he clung so tightly to the wheel, so he let go and ran back to my side of the car.

Professor James quickly started the motor. Red was on the brick sidewalk. The wheels of the right side immediately climbed the curb and he nearly rammed Red into the fence with the front fender. He gunned the motor, jerked the car from the sidewalk and sped down the street with Red in pursuit.

With the car now under control, Professor James ran right through the stop signs of the next two streets and took a right turn without stopping.

"You are married to a madman," he blurted, clearly shaken. "You are coming with me away from him!"

"No, please take me to my sister's house! I will be safe with her," I gasped. I gave him directions over his pleas to go with him.

We arrived at Jennie's, and he waited until I got into the house safely. I just wanted him away from me. This was like a nightmare.

Once inside, at my urging, she turned out the lights. We sat in the dark kitchen with only the street light showing through the windows. If Red came and saw no lights, perhaps he would think I was not there. Additionally, I prayed no one would keep the baby, Teresa, so that he could not look for me.

Jennie and I sat up for a long time, while I explained my dilemma and how I got into it. She was dismayed by the whole situation, frustrated as I.

Waiting until after Red should have gone to work, I took the bus home to not only find our babysitter, Vida, there but also Red. He sent her to the neighbor, Kathleen, to call our employers and say that we were sick. He would not allow me to leave the house, because I told him I would not return when I left again. I had explained over and over that it had been an innocent evening, and further stated that if it was a problem for him I would never return to school. Soon, he told Vida that she could go home for the day.

Then he proceeded to accuse me of having an affair, that he would kill the man. On and on he ranted. Fortunately, the neighbors could not hear. It was beginning to stay cool most of the time, so the windows were down.

He was like a madman, pointing his finger in my face, shaking his fists at me. I asked him what he thought of my waiting for him, night after night, until he decided to come home. Also, that the man would not be stupid enough to let me out in front of the house if there was anything happening between him and me. I kept saying that nothing happened between us, that the man was a gentleman, that I would swear on the life of myself, my baby, and my father that he did not touch me.

By late afternoon, he settled down and was actually talking civil to me. We had dinner and watched some television. In those days the programs were very limited, so we watched the usual show for that night. It was a police show. The plot this night meant disaster for me. In the show, the woman's husband was returning from the service. She had an affair with another man and bore him a child. She had to leave this child on the steps of the police station, so that her returning husband would not know.

Red abruptly cut the TV off before the show ended and began to rant again, "See what a fool she made of him; he trusted her..." On and on the entire evening and all night, he cursed and raved. I would try to get to the door to escape, but there was no such good fortune. He blocked my way. As a skilled fighter and athlete, he knew all the blocks, and one blow from him would have done real damage; his last bouts were heavyweight. I could only let him vent his wrath.

Toward morning, after he attempted to get me to admit a tryst, he began to relax a bit.

So I said, "Please believe me, that I would not allow myself to be dirtied by an affair. That is not my character. My ethics and being an example for my child growing up would not allow this conduct." I even added a favorite, "I don't want to be just another notch on a gun, just another conquest for some man to brag about having."

To this was the addition that if I got out of the house he would never see me again.

After he calmed down and began to be civil, just before morning, he did add that he would kill anybody that got in his way and that I was his wife (chattel, I thought to myself).

He said that neither peace bond that would allow him to only speak to me, nor the other that would not allow him to come near me would make any difference. My fear was indescribable.

Where had the boy, the man that was so caring, tender, loving, promising to protect me, honor me, who never used profanity in front of me, gone?

During this quiet time, my questions were, "Is it my fault that you seem unhappy? Is it the baby? Do you want your freedom to go wherever and whenever you want? Do you resent holding a job and having to pay bills?"

I was physically and mentally exhausted, but I went on, "You do not have to pay a cent of alimony or child support. If freedom is what you want, you may certainly have it with no strings attached. You cannot be happy and be so internally divided and restless as you are, if these things did not make unwelcome demands on you. Please let me go or return to me the same that I give in this marriage!"

He went on to plead forgiveness for doubting me, that he loved Teresa and me and would be lost without us. Because there had been no rest for either of us when

Vida came in for work, he had her call our employers to say we were ill again. The day was peaceful; we rested, but I was uneasy, wondering about the future.

We managed to work things out and about a year later, our second girl, Robin was born. We had moved to the outskirts of Nashville, called the Bordeaux area. Never had I been without a full-time job since graduation; this time it was no different. We lived within view of the Bordeaux Bridge, and the Cumberland River was behind us. At the edge of the yard was a steep drop down to the deep muddy waters. Teresa was cautioned not to go near that edge. She never did, thank God (I say reverently)!

Church attendance since I married had been erratic, I seldom went. My faith was unwavering, but I felt that all who knew me could see in my eyes that I questioned my situation at home and was not happy. I abhorred pity, so I avoided seeing many friends. I'm sure they raised the same mental question as I did about our marriage: Was it true love or just physical attraction? My sincere vows were to be true, until death do us part, but he wasn't keeping up his end of the contract, and he acknowledged it often when asking my forgiveness for his excessive drinking, gambling with money we could not spare, and staying out until all hours of the night. This was not my idea of a fair marriage, much less a good, sensible marriage.

Most of the time, a trek up the (no sidewalk) street was my way to catch the bus that crossed the bridge to take me to downtown Nashville to my bank job. This also was my way home, except for an occasional ride by Red.

On occasion, when I did go to church on Sunday, he dropped me off and later picked me up, never going himself. Liquor was heavy on his breath, letting me know this was how he spent his time during my absence. An argument usually ensued giving him an excuse to angrily exit the house, not to return until late Sunday night. I guess I thought that these episodes would not happen if I stayed home and watched him. My confusion was getting worse by the day. Where were we going on this path we were on?

To go to church on Sunday, feel so peaceful, so serene, and then come home to a fracas was disconcerting to me. Why go on?

Often, my thoughts were of leaving him. A visit to an attorney did no good except to get another couple of weeks of cooperation out of him and artificial promises.

I had tried everything: To be a good cook and housekeeper, to avoid arguments, to allow him more time with his friends, to be his lover, mistress, to seduce him; the whole gamut, but nothing seemed to change. One day, I realized he would never grow up and assume responsibilities; it was out of his realm.

Leaving him was my only solution. A phone call to a familiar moving company was my out. They were instructed to be at my house about 30 minutes after he departed for work on the specified day. They knew him, knew his temper, so they listened carefully to my timing. They were to get every piece of furniture and my belongings out and be completely out of sight before noon, since he often came home for lunch. That day he left for work early, leaving me, as usual, getting ready to go to the bus to work. I got ready for work, but waited for the moving men. Once there, I hurried them to load. The house was completely empty before noon. Then I went up to the highway and got the bus, arriving at work late, of course, part of my preplanning.

Later, I learned that he went into the house at lunch, his mouth dropped when he saw there was no furniture and no one home. Nothing, nobody there—zilch.

My abode was a boarding house in the West area, while family took care of Teresa and Robin. My exit from work was to ride to the bus line, crouching down in the back of a coworker's car. Before leaving work, I had gone to the front of the bank and observed him across the street. He thought he was hidden as he waited for me to leave work, apparently baffled that he could not intercept me.

This went on for several days. Then our pastor phoned from the church. Red had been there on his knees crying, begging him to get me to return. Since his behavior had been so well hidden from others by me, I relented and returned to him, because there was no financial way to make it alone with two babies.

Mother Nola suggested an apartment in an older house across the street from her. She recommended that we move there so that she could continue to keep the children during the day while we worked.

Prior to that, we had moved several times, the last being a room with her. She had girl boarders in the tri-level house, so she let us have a room, including meals, for a small fee. This enormous gesture was to help us get financially able to survive alone. Meals were cooked by her, a maid, and a daughter who also had her husband and children there. Red privately told me within a few weeks that he felt smothered and did not want to live like this, that we were to get out. (This was his excuse to keep Mother Nola and Papa from knowing about his flagrant behavior.)

We moved into the apartment across the street from Mother Nola.

My husband's idea of pleasing the children was different than mine. For example: he brought home a live baby goat to the small apartment. The goat was definitely a smash with the girls; they loved to hold it and feed it with a baby bottle that he had brought along with the goat. My questions to him after the initial shock were: Where will the goat sleep? Who will keep it during the day? What about the mess from not being potty trained? What to do when it grows up, especially since we were in the city with no fence?

After getting no answers to my questions and threatening to leave him if the goat stayed, he announced to the children that they would have to go with him and give it to someone else (sucker). They began a duet of crying; Mama was cruel, and the goat would not have a home. They pleaded with me while he looked on. Within minutes, they were out the door with it but still crying because Mama would not relent.

Each morning, I took the children over to my stepmother's house so I could go to work. She charged us nothing and always invited us to dinner without charge. Truly, she was a saint. One night, an hour past my normal time to get the children, I asked Red to take the children home because I had something to discuss with her. I broke down and wept when we reached the privacy of her bedroom.

Distraught, I asked, "Mother Nola, remember the ghastly episode with the professor? Please, would you tell me what to do about this?"

"Clara, whatever it is, you know my advice will be what is best for you. What has happened?"

Papa came in, "Am I interrupting something?" He noted my crying, for sure.

"Ross, will you excuse us? It's about Clara's job," she answered. His aging was quite apparent; but his ability to handle what little he learned about my tempestuous marriage was good, unless he hid his feelings well. He slowly left the room.

"Mother Nola," I shook as I spoke, unable to stop. "I was called into Mr. L's office to take a letter. Everyone else was gone. Knowing Red was outside in the pickup, waiting for me, I asked if I could take the letter down and type it the next morning. He said I could do that and pointed to the pullout at his desk for my tablet. I sat down in the chair under the pullout. It was by the door he had just closed.

Mr. L dictated a letter, one that did not seem that important to me. He asked me to read it back, which I did. He then leaned over me, asking a question I did not understand. He was standing to my right side; I looked up to ask him what he had said and he came down on my lips and kissed me and, before I could get up, he brushed his hand on my left breast.

"Mother Nola, I was sick with embarrassment, got up quickly and got out of there, not remembering what I said to him. My mind was in a spin. This man who got his nails manicured every Friday, friend of political heavies, well respected, married with children. Is this the real world, and I'm not ready for it? What do I do? In the truck, I told Red I didn't feel well. That was most certainly the truth. He believed me.

"Do I just not go back to work? I cannot be normal around him again. Surely the man and the other lady in the office will note the change in my disposition. How could he do such a thing?" I asked as my frustration grew.

"Clara, you go to him and tell him you are not that kind of person. Tell him right away! Put him in his place, and I'm sure this will not happen again. Let me know what happens. But don't tell Raymond (Red)!" That last bit of advice was to prevent trouble from Red.

"Thank you, Mother Nola. The first time he is in the office and the others are gone, he will be told."

Sure enough, that time came within days. Every time he came near me, I would take a step back even if employees and customers were present. I dreaded going to work. Once he softly said to me, "Why do you step back from me when I approach you?" I pretended not to hear.

Alone at my typewriter on a Friday shortly after my talk with Mother Nola, Mr. L came out of his office. Without looking up from my typewriter, I blurted, "About the other day in your office, I don't know what ever gave you the idea that I was that kind of person. Do you want me to quit?"

He answered as if surprised, "I didn't mean anything by it. I'm sorry the incident upset you; you don't have to avoid me."

I retorted by saying, "I certainly hope my husband doesn't go around greeting women like that, and saying he meant nothing by it."

Soon thereafter, nausea abounded, but I associated it with the stress of my job. Instead, I was pregnant with Susan, my third daughter. One Friday Mr. L went out to his usual lunch. Immediately after his departure, I went home for lunch and did not return. My resignation, put on his desk before leaving, stated that it was because of ill health. This type of departure was abrupt and unprofessional, but I felt it was appropriate under the circumstances. He telephoned several weeks later and asked if my testimony would be available regarding a lawsuit by his relatives suing to get part of the company. My reply was, "Mr. C came into the office many times. He used an abundance of profanity, but was a perfect gentleman around me." The statement was made as an insinuation that he did not measure up to the compliment I had just paid his brother.

A quick apology ensued for having bothered me; there was never any further contact with me. (According to the newspaper the next year, he committed suicide. My prayers were for his soul; he must have been an unhappy man.)

CHAPTER 7

Realizing that Red's income was far from sufficient, Mother Nola suggested to me that a boarding house would be an income for my little family. Since Susan was on the way, outside work was out of the question for me. She set about to find a house big enough for the business. Of course Red and I had no money for a down payment, extra furniture, and the other multiple associated needs. Not to worry, she said. As usual, she was right. Within weeks, we moved into a vacant, one-floor nursing home in East Nashville. I was elated with the purchase made with Mother Nola's help.

Red and I would occupy the bedroom next to the huge kitchen that also served as the dining room. The children occupied the oversized bedroom next to us. The house reeked with the smell of urine. Again, she said not to worry. She came over with Papa and began to lay new linoleum in the back hall and kitchen, paint the wallpaper and woodwork, while Papa looked after Teresa and Robin. With new paint covering the walls and plenty of scrubbing of the floors, the house was transformed.

Mother Nola and Papa would spend about three days with me, then return to her boarding house for the four remaining days of each week until the house was ready for boarders. She alone did most of the labor to accomplish this. Because of my pregnancy, my labor was limited to duties away from the paint, climbing the ladders, or other dangerous tasks. Papa's declining health also prevented him from helping, but he could watch the children. This angelic woman was my stepmother, and I loved and appreciated her very much. Over and over, many times, I reminded her of my appreciation of her many displays of love for us.

The bank held the first mortgage. Because Mother Nola had done so much business with the real estate lady who sold me the house, she took her commission by the month from me, until paid in full. This was a second mortgage.

The purchase of beds, chests of drawers, and other furniture for my boarders, was backed up by Mother Nola's word. She took me to a furniture store where she had been a longtime customer. They extended credit with no problem.

The bed linens were furnished by the laundry company she patronized. Boarders came from the two business colleges that provided her with female boarders. Her recommendation of me was adequate for the schools.

There were approximately nine girls occupying my dorm-like bedrooms. The entrance hall was the living room for us all.

Vida was hired to help me. We cleaned the main areas, and the girls cleaned their own rooms. Vida prepared the meats and vegetables; I made the desserts and beverages.

Recipes for volume came from Mother Nola. Vida worked five days a week, coming in at seven a.m. Alone, I prepared breakfast seven days a week for the boarders and my family, a fast food type of dinner on Saturday night, and only breakfast on Sunday.

When I went into labor, Mother Nola took Teresa and Robin to stay with her for the week, until I could work again. Vida took care of the boarders until I came home with the new baby. But while staying with Mother Nola, Teresa and Robin got the mumps and had to stay an additional week. My apologies were many, but it was a blessing for me to have an extra week to recuperate and prepare myself for my duties and this additional baby to nurture. Teresa was three and a half years old, Robin was one and a half, and now Susan was here.

Red continued to work for the city as an assistant water meter reader. He seemed to be calming down more. His drinking was limited. There were even days that he played with the children and took them to the park. On weekends, we sometimes churned homemade ice cream on our back steps.

My children were a delight to the neighbors. Across the street were three elderly people, a brother and two sisters. They often told me that my house provided their entertainment, especially the children. Often the postman would take a shortcut across the yard and chat with the children, when they were allowed on the front porch.

Robin loved her coat; she would put it on in July, be barefooted, and Teresa would stand alongside her and sing loudly the popular song of the day, "Davy, Davy Fockitt, King of the Wild Fonteeerr (Davy, Davy Crockett, King of the Wild Frontier)." This mispronunciation of her words amused the neighbors. She always wore her cowboy boots. One of us would be near to be sure they did not leave the porch.

Eighteen months after Susan was born, Lisa, my fourth daughter was born. All my deliveries had been difficult, but I survived.

Teresa was the perfect little lady, never setting foot over any boundaries drawn for her. Robin was the traveler (this would prove true also in later years). There was no exit from their bedroom, except through the door into our bedroom. This led to the kitchen, and Vida and I were usually there. When they were playing in their room, a folding gate across the open door provided security.

One fall day, Robin eluded me as I busied myself with Susan and other duties in the house.

By this time, we had changed boarders (at Red's insistence since he was disturbed by the traffic of the boyfriends of the girl boarders we previously had there). The young men were students from the auto diesel college in our area of town. This meant the boys stayed in their rooms more than girls. Also, they went out to call on their dates. (As for me, I was happy with them all.)

The young men boarders were a total of nine, but others heard about how much they enjoyed living with us and five more requested that they be residents. This meant that their cots were crowded more like military style; but they did not mind at all. We furnished them with good meals, changed their linens once a week, and then they cared for their rooms the rest of the week, just as the girls had done. Most went to their hometowns for the weekends. Some were from rural communities and other states, while some had been in the military.

This additional group meant that 14 lunches had to be prepared each morning for them to brown-bag to school.

About Robin and her wanderlust: Teresa came and said Robin was not in her room. Vida and I searched the house and yard, calling frantically. No answer. (Once we had caught her climbing over the back fence in the yard, not too far from their playground equipment. Red added to the gate's height, and built the fence higher on each side of the gate. She was always trying to loosen the planks of the picket fence to crawl through. Until Red nailed each plank tightly, she was successful in calling on the neighbors when my back was turned. Then there was the time my phone rang; a neighbor stopped her as she was going into the grocery through the swinging door. The grocery was on the corner, a block away. Then, there was the time she dug under the back fence. Vida and I watched until she huffed and puffed through the hole she had just made, then we quietly went through the gate and stood there with crossed arms and greeted her when she came up on the other side.)

The police and Red were yet to be called. Our diaper delivery man drove up and asked what the problem was. After hysterically telling him what had happened and that Robin was missing, he jumped back into his truck, saying that he would circle the blocks, and he sped off.

By this time, Red had been contacted on his job and the police were on the way. Before either arrived, the diaper delivery man returned with Robin in the truck. He had found her several blocks away, across busy Shelby Avenue, sitting down watching several workmen build a barn. They told him she arrived earlier and wondered where she had come from. He hastily got her back to me.

We put the hooks higher on the doors, but she would get the broom and unlock them. She was definitely "a miniature escape artist," I often quipped when she was not around.

The young boarders often complimented the children, saying they were so good; that unless they saw them, they did not know small children were in the house. This pleased me, because they seldom cried or had reason to cry.

Going downtown with four children by myself was difficult to say the least. One such necessary trip was to a well-known shoe store. They were having a summer sale. Vida and I got the children ready and then alone, I took them all on the bus expecting to buy four pairs of new shoes. On reaching the store, a line of waiting mothers and children extended out the door and down the sidewalk. At one glance, I concluded that buying shoes for these four could not be accomplished. So, with Susan's hand in mine, Robin on a leash, Lisa under one arm, and Teresa walking along beside me, we headed back home—with no shoes. We had a little more than a city block to walk to get the bus. Upon passing a parked car with two laughing men inside, they called out to me, asking what I was doing with so many children.

Immediately, I recognized them as old school friends. It was good to see them. They had seen the five of us coming, recognized and waited for me, watching me struggle down the street with my little entourage.

The young men boarders were happy with us, and they often told me so. We were happy to have them. The house note and mortgages were paid. There was always food in the house.

The baby, Lisa, was getting along well, and so were the other three children. Red seemed to take the responsibility of the boarders in stride. At last all seemed well, with a stable future in sight for us.

Then one night Red dropped a bomb.

"Clara, sit down on the bed beside me and let's talk about something!" The older children were outside playing on the swing set and Lisa was asleep in her crib; it was about dusk.

"I want to open a tavern on Charlotte in West Nashville. You have met Shorty. He will run it in the daytime, and I will help him after leaving work every day of the week. I will take it on Saturdays and Sundays, too. Mr. J., the jukebox man, will finance me. He will put the pinball machine, jukebox, and shuffleboard in at no cost to me. He will take the money from the machines and give me a percentage of the take. Beer and other profits will be mine alone. Also, he will provide the furniture, which will fall in with my building rent. I can really make some money. It's a good location." His enthusiastic demeanor was sincere. He clutched my hands tightly. His eyes pleaded with me for approval.

My heart sank. We were paying our bills and buying a home. Wasn't that enough?

"I have wanted to tell you for a long time that I don't like all these people in my house, minding my business. The boarders will have to go. Please, honey! You won't have to do anything except mind the house and take care of the children. Don't you get tired of all this work, and so many people in the house?" He frowned as he spoke.

"Red you know I don't approve of the sale of any form of liquor, because so many people tend to abuse it. Just as my grandfather said, there are men who hang around a place like that when they should be home with their wives and children. If all people drank in moderation, I certainly would not object; but they don't." I looked away as I continued, so that he could not see the distress that surely must have been on my face.

"This is disturbing to me. Excessive drinking has broken up so many homes, including our own many times. If you insist on making this move, please don't ask me to say yes or no. If I say yes, and you fail, you would say that I could have stopped you. If I say no, you will accuse me of trying to keep you from making money. So, this must be your decision alone," I said.

When Red made a decision, it had to be his way or not at all. Within a few days, he excitedly came into the house, pulled me aside and asked that Ethel (our new housekeeper) stay overtime so he could drive me out to the tavern. The day I dreaded had really come to fruition. Soon, I announced to the young men that the house would be closed except to the family. It was nearly time for their graduation anyway, so no one was inconvenienced.

Vida had earlier secured a job with the state, which was pleasing to me. Her abilities far exceeded my job requirements. After Vida's departure, Ethel had come aboard and was doing a fine job as well. It was difficult for me to tell her she was no longer needed.

Mother Nola and I quietly agreed the whole thing was not a good idea. Neither of us expressed our honest opinions to Red, for fear of creating a disturbance.

Red did not close the tavern until late at night, so he was ready to go to sleep once he got home. The children were already asleep. He left for his day job as they got up. The weekends were the same; they seldom saw him.

While the boarders were with us and, now, with so many work hours per day taking up his time, Red drank far less than the years before. This was a blessing for him, our marriage, our children and me. A few months later, his business became erratic; it began to lose money, and he said we would have to leave the house and go rent again. My worst fears were now realized. We sold the house and moved near Mother Nola and Vanderbilt University.

I went to work on the campus at Vanderbilt as the secretary for an entire department, consisting of 13 professors. They were kind and wonderful employers. In addition to being the only secretary in the building, I was also librarian for half a day in between my other duties. Miss Bev was librarian during the first half of the day.

One day the children and I developed strep throat. A nurse came to the house on Friday and gave us shots. On Monday, I walked across the campus to the hospital, relating to the doctor that I had started bleeding in the bathroom on the first floor, and that I was weak climbing the stairs to work that morning. He concluded that I had spontaneously aborted my fifth child that morning in the restroom. After examinations by other residents/ interns, it was definite that I had lost my fetus. A dilatation and curettage was done. What on earth could I have done with another child? The nightmares ahead would be more burdensome with another mouth to feed. This attitude may have seemed calloused to some, but to me it was relief. Lisa was not yet a year old.

Things weren't going well with Red, and again, we separated. I was back on the marriage "roller coaster." (My relatives must, by now, consider me insane.) My job was at Vanderbilt, and my saintly stepmother offered me residence in her home again. (She had earlier moved her boarding business closer to Vanderbilt after selling her previous home.) She also volunteered to keep the children while I worked. We would occupy the tiny screened-in sun-porch at the rear of the house.

It was tremendously difficult for her. Though she had a maid, the burden of the household and my father fell on her shoulders. One day there was a personal call to me at work from a relative that the arrangement was taking a toll on Mother Nola. They requested that we move out as soon as possible. Mother Nola knew nothing of the call to me, and objected to my decision to go.

Red had been calling me every day, begging me to return to him. This time there was no choice for me. He met me at the local park. We would leave town and start life afresh, he promised. He was giving up the tavern and would accept a job offer in Miami, Florida, hauling kosher chickens from Indiana.

CHAPTER 8

We went to Miami with only Robin, via bus, leaving the other three children with Mother Nola and Papa. They would stay with them until we found living quarters. When we arrived in Miami after that exhausting bus ride, his new boss loaned him a truck for personal use. The previous one that we owned was too much in disrepair to make such a long trip and Red sold it before the trip from Nashville.

We located a house after several days. In searching for rentals, we would see a yard sign, knock on the door, and answer their questions. Once the owners found out that we had four small children, it seemed they could not get the door shut fast enough. One would have thought we were bringing a circus to town to occupy the unit.

Fortunately, his new boss was from Nashville and was an old friend of his; he let us stay with him while we searched for a house or apartment. After constantly searching, from morning to night, we rented a house in a semi-industrial area.

We returned to Nashville and could take only as much furniture as the small truck's bed would allow. The six of us sat in the cab, closely packed. On the way there, Red was running out of money, so we picked up a huge bag of broken cookies at a bakery. With an occasional cup of coffee (Red and I would split), milk for baby Lisa and rationed milk for the other three girls, that was our only nourishment. We feared running out of gas in the Everglades area.

The children's biological clocks were different, so potty breaks were often. When we piled out of the small truck cab, I imagined the onlookers must have said, "Look at that poor white trash!"

By the time we reached Miami, we had only one dollar. Red forgot which street we were to turn off on to get to our new residence. Our gas was getting low. Then he recognized a car repair shop on the main street that ran behind our house. Red had put food in the house before we left, so we knew we were going to be fed.

After we ate, we all fell exhausted into our beds.

The grueling task while on our initial trip (carrying Robin with us) of going from door to door, street by street, to find a place to live, was tiring. Because we were on a deadline it did not leave us the option of examining our living quarters, nor to be selective. We were forced to take anything we were offered. Our time was running out. We had to get back to Nashville to get the children so that Red could earn some money for our living expenses.

The next morning on opening the jalousies (the horizontal slats that would admit air and sun, but exclude the rain), I noted they were all metal. The wire screens on these windows had holes in them. To my horror, they would admit mosquitoes easily, as well as numerous flies that would appear during the day and especially at night. There was no glass covering either window. My little ones were subject to irritation as well as serious disease. Before breakfast, I set about to stuff each hole with tissue.

This meant that when it rained and closing of the jalousies was necessary, all daylight would be shut out. We didn't have a fan or other cooling system. Therefore, it was hot and sultry inside. While Red was gone on his first trip to Indiana, the water backed up in all our plumbing. There was no telephone. Fortunately, the landlady happened by, so this was remedied.

Red got back from his first round trip to Indiana without having slept, except for the short time they were loading the chickens for his return trip. When he got home, he laid down across the bed to rest, as I prepared his food. Fortunately, he had stripped his clothes down to his underwear before he fell asleep. When I tried to awaken him for his dinner, I was repulsed to see that he had chicken lice on his legs. Apparently, he was too tired to notice the lice. I could not get him to wake up. What to do? He simply should not have to tolerate those things on him. So, I got his shaving brush, soap-lathered his legs and shaved them off.

Soon, I got a job with a correspondence school. It was a combination secretary and bookkeeping job, within other schools under the same roof, all separate partnerships with the same president (the initial owner and family). By the time my babysitter was paid, my salary netted about $30 per week. At work, I gave some advice on problem areas, resulting in all overtime being cut out. Because of this, a bonus of two week's salary was given to me. The job was a challenge, and it was enjoyable.

The beach proved to be fun for the whole family. Red would often get home early, prepare sandwiches, get the children, pick me up after work, and we would play in the water until bedtime.

We shortly moved into a downstairs apartment that housed four families on the first floor and four on the second. We lived on the first floor.

Later, we moved for the third time to another house that was nearer to my job.

For recreation, we often rode down the street next to the beach, watching the activity. Once we passed the hotel where we were told Frank Sinatra was filming, "A Hole in the Head," I think it was titled.

The miles of hotels and beach fronts were unbelievable. A suntan was out of the question for my skin, so the rays were limited for me. Since Red and I were fair skinned, the girls were limited to exposure but they seemed to fare better than we did. There were always fresh fruits and vegetables for us to enjoy.

Subsequent to half a dozen trips to Kentucky, my travels had only been in Tennessee, so Miami seemed to be far, far away from Nashville. My letters and communications with my families had always been brief and limited so that they would not perceive my seesaw marriage... especially Red's erratic behavior. Moving to Miami was no different. My letters were always aglow with our healthy children, my job, and scantily about his jobs (they varied as well in Miami). At least there were no hints for them to worry about me... I had caused them enough grief.

When he exhibited signs of falling back into his old habits, I went to free counseling, just as I had in Nashville. He refused to go, saying that he did not need any help and that he was happy. This attitude repulsed me. Was it that he feared someone outside would uncover his real motives and temperament? Was he hiding something? (My feelings were that all people need to look inside themselves, analyze their behavior, and determine how to communicate with other human beings in a positive manner. Sometimes, we all need help in discerning our attitudes and behaviors.)

Many times when the children were outside playing, and he was gone, I would be washing the dishes or making the beds with tears streaming down my face, singing, "I'll Take You Home Again, Kathleen." My heart was broken. I missed home, my relatives and friends so very much. Why did I have to leave and move so far away just so that he could begin anew? Apparently the influence of his friends was not the sole cause of his "juvenile" behavior and his inability to accept responsibility as a grown man.

In my despair, I would pray, "God, what bad thing did I ever do to deserve this?" (In my rational moments, I realized this question was self-centered and childish.) And looking back, could I have depended on myself too much to solve the problems?

Though I tried to get Red to take us to church, he would not hear of it. "Why not?" was always my question verbally and to myself.

There was an ad in the newspaper that caught my attention: a house available in the suburbs that could be purchased with no down payment. Just take over the existing notes. It was a comfortable corner house, with a grass-covered lawn for the children. The floors were terrazo, easy for me to clean, there were three bedrooms, large kitchen, a bath for us and one for the children. It seemed too good to be true. Within days, we were in that lovely house. Red was back to selling produce but, in Miami, it wasn't quite as seasonal. There was usually something growing in all seasons that was marketable. My ride to work was with a neighbor who lived a couple of blocks away. The fee he charged me paid for the gas in the car. His name was Jack and he was a former crop duster. Sometimes he drove with the abandon of flying alone in the sky but, in reality, it was the highway. His wife was a schoolteacher. They were a lovely couple. He worked in my office, so getting to work on time was always his goal, too.

Eventually the profit margin for Red began to sink. Too, he took the liberty of drinking at the taverns when business was slack. That habit, plus the sinking funds for house expenses and food, led him to imbibe even more. What to do now?

As previously mentioned, there were four schools within our office owned by four men and Mr. Mack. He was also president and part owner of each school. One day Mr. Mack fired five of the ladies that worked for the other schools. I never learned the reason for the firings. He gave me the extra work to oversee, keep up to date, and train the new personnel coming in to replace them. Somehow, I got it done.

One day the boss of the school for which I worked came in from his southern region. He asked if my family would move to Shreveport, Louisiana, which was his home, and take charge of his office. Red said, "Why not? If he will pay our moving expenses." We were already behind with our house notes.

Papa had died, just months before. When word came from my family, my telegram back to them was that I would not be there and to go on with the funeral without me. This was heartbreaking. My instructions to my bosses at work were not to tell anyone the real reason for my three day absence. Sympathy would have been intense and sincere and would have made my grief more profound. The office thought my absence was from illness. Within months, my sister, Donie, died as a result of a house fire. Again, I could not go home because there was absolutely no money for the long trip, and who would mind the children?

Leaving Florida, Red drove the truck with our few possessions through a breathtaking area. Gratefully, we relished the smell of the miles and miles of orange groves. Then, when we reached Mississippi, all along the coastal area, the beauty of the magnificent blooms of the azaleas delighted us. The ride was a never-to-be-forgotten journey. In Shreveport, Mr. M had rented us a comfortable, roomy apartment in a lovely neighborhood. Mrs. M was there to see that we were settled in quickly. All of our expenses to get there and to set up were taken care of by Mrs. M.

After a few days, she took me to the office to show me around. While there, Mr. M said my move was to actually run the operation of his own correspondence school that he was forming. The school would be about credit and finance. My salary was increased considerably, compared to my meager previous salary. The salesmen were from the Miami school, but scattered in different states.

CHAPTER 9

The course was written by a prominent university dean. He would dictate the lessons, and my secretary would transcribe them. Then I would read them, make necessary corrections, and mail them back to him for final approval. After editing, he would return them to me. I would then take them to the illustrator, then to the printer. Each printed lesson was assembled by my office, and then mailed to the students.

Things went well until it was necessary for me to work overtime. When Red came to the office for me, he expected me to immediately quit work for the day. He felt that eight hours were enough.

After a few months, he demanded that I resign and get a "real" job. His reasoning made no sense whatsoever; but arguing only made matters worse. Shortly, I resigned and, because of my being the central person with the ability to cover all bases, Mr. M closed the school. He was in the oil business and stood to inherit several oil fields, so the school investment was not that important to him.

He spent more time buying oil leases and oil rights than he did with the school. At that time, it seemed that there were more oil rigs than trees covering the ground around Shreveport and into East Texas. Miles and miles of oil rigs spread over the land. Quite a different landscape change for a girl from Tennessee.

Just prior to my resignation, I talked to Red about AA (Alcoholics Anonymous). He declared that he had no problem. With this attitude, all seemed hopeless.

After secretly renting an apartment and telling Mr. and Mrs. M that my marriage had always been in trouble, I took the children and moved out on him. It was humiliating and embarrassing to have to explain all of this to them.

The apartment was on the opposite side of town. We thought we were safe there, at least for a while, hoping he would come to his senses. Through friends, we learned that he was desperately looking for us. This was a repeat of his usual behavior each time I left him.

A lovely, older couple that had been our neighbors before we left Red, suggested that they intercede and try to get him to Alcoholics Anonymous. This precious couple told me that they had met at an AA meeting and married shortly thereafter. For many years, they had been and were active, ardent supporters of the organization. I asked them to go to him, to not mention having had any contact with us, and suggest that maybe we would return if he gave up his drinking and abuse that went along with the madness.

They called me the next evening, saying that he had agreed to go. Red did not know they knew of my whereabouts. Mr. B told me that he would be going with him at 6:30 p.m. the next day. He told me the location. The irony of the meeting place: it was directly across the street from our apartment, and we could watch them enter. What a coincidence! Of all the streets in Shreveport, it would be our street. (I often wondered about the busy house across the street with cars and people going and coming. It had no sign on it.)

At the appointed time, the children came in from play. From our living room window, we watched Mr. B's car go into the driveway across the street. Red was on the passenger side of the car, and we saw him. Every time he came to a meeting, they would phone me to keep the children inside so that he would not spot us. We were astonished that AA was on our street.

The children giggled with glee, commenting that "Daddy would be surprised to know we stand at the window and watch them go into his meeting... that we are this near to him." We were careful to keep the blinds partially closed.

Days passed. The B's told me he was miserable alone, and asked if a reconciliation could be worked out. Mrs. B suggested that my attendance at Al-Anon (dependents of alcoholics) could possibly help.

The children begged to see their father; they could only see fun and games with him. I was the serious one, who thought about paying the rent, buying food, paying the electric bill, buying their clothes and seeing to the "dull stuff."

We returned to him in a few days after he sincerely promised to do better, to abandon his bad behavior, and to continue to go to AA. In quiet moments, I would look him squarely in the eyes and ask him if he was unhappy with me, was there someone else he preferred, or did he resent that we took his freedom? Further, if he wanted to be free of us, he could be, with no strings attached. I would not ask him for child support or alimony of any kind, and he could see the children anytime he wanted. Just leave me alone to live in peace with the children. Or please give me some stability in my marriage, if we were to continue to live together. I would emphasize that I was sincere and not to treat the matter lightly. He would laugh as if the subject was trivial. (I had said these same things, many times before. Would this time be any different?)

The AA meetings were so informative. We met all together in a large room, attended by about 50 people, then we would separate and Al-Anon would go to another room. No one gave last names. We shared our experiences, as much as we felt comfortable telling. This went on for several meetings, then he said that the smoking at the coffee fellowship bothered him, and he did not want to go back. What a flimsy excuse, I thought. True, neither of us ever smoked, but it did not bother me. The apparent and anticipated good results were worth any inconvenience to me. It was such a small sacrifice, to get the knowledge and camaraderie of these people, and to try to make our marriage work. It was no secret that he apparently wanted to return to the bottle.

Another house and another job later, I fell on a throw rug in the den. On falling, the left knee was clearly heard crunching. The pain was excruciating. The left knee had been jumping out of place daily ever since the fall, when I was five years old. I depended on the right knee for security. It had taken severe punishment from the hundreds of falls brought about by the left knee.

After the rug fall in the den, I visited the orthopedic doctor and he said the left knee had been severely damaged. If the operation was not done now, then I would be limping by Easter. This was early spring. Before my nerve was lost, I told him to operate. When I woke he told me the patella was taken out permanently. Because of the wear and tear on it, there was only a third of the kneecap left, not enough to save.

The leg would be housed in a cast and necessitate a wheelchair and crutches again.

The children were wonderful to me. They took over house duties, as well as their young minds and hands could perform. I could see they were beginning to comprehend more the violent temper of their father. So many years of trying to protect them, to hide and shush his tirades from them were now in the past. They were old enough to fear him.

The disarming thing to us all was the charm he could demonstrate, the fun he could be, and promises that seemed so sincere, finally seeing the light of kindness, love, and the rewards of peace and tranquility. Who was this man, who showed a different side to us and another outside the home? Outside was not always tranquil either when he would fight in a saloon over some slight look or remark that was made that he did not like.

My vacation and sick time were used for the operation and recovery. This was limited, so I had to return before the cast was off. A taxi was my conveyance, and the waste can under my desk kept my leg propped up during the day.

After the cast was removed, a very kind lady came by the office at the insistence of my doctor. She told me she had the same operation from a fall that broke her kneecap. The operation was a success and, with no kneecap, she was now playing nine holes of golf as often as she liked. The doctor must have sensed my despair and wanted me to know that "this, too, will pass," a favorite old saying of mine that had seen me through many crises. Her operation had been done only the year before.

One evening Red came home inebriated. I was still in the cast. He ranted on and on, often coming to the bedside and pointing his finger in my face for emphasis about senseless issues. I began to have muscle spasms, apparently inside the cast; my leg would shake and then jerk. They were so violent from my nervous state, I was sure the lower part of my leg would dangle from the knee when the cast came off. He soon calmed down enough to give me the telephone to call the doctor for some pain pills to stop the spasms. The children fled the house and spent the night in the open church bus that was parked a few houses up the street. Apparently he thought they had gone to bed. After he got the pills for me, he went to sleep. Peace at last.

Often, the desire to get away, far, far away, would dominate my daydreams. How could this be accomplished? To get far enough away that we would be safe from him, and give him the freedom to live his life as he wished, was my goal.

In the interim, before the operation, we had lived in another part of the city. There, one semester of college was possible for me, courtesy of a grant and a small loan. My job would allow me to work around my hours required at the college. It was difficult, necessitating that I rise at three a.m. to get my studying in, but each course was passed. This was an experiment by me to see if I could do it. The college was close enough to walk home after class, but the bus was my transportation from work to my classes, and also to work each day.

In order to keep my sanity, prayer was necessary and welcome. The continuous mental plot to get the children and me as many miles away as possible one day was my objective, my only hope.

Teresa was the eldest and could see the insanity of our existence more than the others, as clearly as her young mind could comprehend. He seemed to snipe at her the most. She never seemed to please him anymore, no matter what she did. One evening during dinner at the small kitchen table, she was her usual quiet self. She had become used to staring down at her plate during mealtime.

Red snapped, "What's the matter with you? Sit up!"

She brought her eyes slowly up to him, with no expression to cause ire, not saying anything. She sat up, going on with her meal, hardly eating.

He suddenly threw his plastic drinking glass across the table, and it broke on her forehead. I jumped up in horror, not knowing what damage had been done to her. Fortunately, she was not hurt.

The children had two parakeets—a male and female. In another illogical fit of rage, he threw the cage containing them across the room, killing the male.

The usual punishments for the children for what I felt were minor infractions were met with a thrashing with his waist belt. When this was done, I would rub the welts and cry, usually after he had stomped out of the house in his rage. Another time he put his fist through the wall. To hide this from anyone coming in, I hung a picture over the hole.

From there we moved again to a house which would prove to be our last with Red.

My job was with an electrical company. They did wiring for commercial businesses. On the corner from the company was a small family-owned café where I sometimes lunched. When Red was late picking me up, he knew to drive up to the café, where I would sit, nursing a cup of coffee, watching out the window. I waited there many an hour or more when he dawdled in picking me up. It was understood that I could wait any length of time for him, but I was to be prompt in being outside when my workday was over.

The important thing to me was to keep the children and me from getting hurt until I could devise a way of escape from this marriage.

Mrs. L, the owner, would often sit with me in the café and talk. She could clearly see that Red was often tipsy when he was late coming for me. After several weeks, she began to subtly ask questions. My answers were, as usual, guarded until I felt the person was not going to use the information to pity me or gossip.

Almost at once, I knew she was a good friend to have.

One day she mentioned she and her husband were going to Kansas City to buy an additional restaurant. I cannot remember the reason why that particular location (Kansas City) was wanted by them.

On hearing this, my mind began to wonder if this lady could be my exit to freedom. At home, when alone, I got a map and began to study the area, and to read up on the state of Missouri. Noting that the University of Missouri was in Columbia, between Kansas City and St. Louis, I felt Columbia would be a wonderful place to settle down.

The children, hopefully, could go to college on grants, and I could furnish their living quarters. Knowing my income would never allow for their higher education, this would be the best bet. Too, they could walk from their home to the University, thereby not needing an expense such as a car. Surely they could work on weekends and earn book money.

Then I borrowed a Dun & Bradstreet book from a neighbor, to see what businesses were there that would allow me a job.

Our neighbors had always been exceptionally friendly to all of us. One neighbor had been present and caught a glimmer of Red's temper with the children and me a couple of times. These times, she immediately excused herself and went home. Her husband knew him, too, occasionally running into him at the local bar and grill, and having a beer with him. In confidence to her, I disclosed my desire to leave him permanently. She understood and vowed not to relate anything to her husband, who might accidentally let the information slip during one of his casual encounters with Red at the bar.

She had a breathing problem that caused her much distress. When she had an attack, I would have her call Teresa to sit with her until it was over. She was so grateful for Teresa's help. This proved helpful also to Teresa and me. When Red would burst into a tantrum, I would quickly ring her and whisper into the phone, "Call Teresa!" Then, I would distance myself from the phone and wait that few seconds for it to ring. Usually Teresa was backed into a distant room being belted. I would, of course, answer the phone, rush in and tell him to let Teresa go, that Mrs. N was having a life-threatening attack. Miraculously, it worked.

Red never refused to let Teresa go to help Mrs. N. Her husband thanked Red many times in public for Teresa's needed help. (He never knew about the "false alarms" his wife conjured up for Teresa's rescue.) Thank God (I say this reverently)!

How many times did this dear lady save her from severe undeserved punishment (perhaps, Teresa's life) and calm the raging bull?

Because my mind was made up to escape, I turned to the little church near us and made an appointment to see the pastor. I blurted out my story, that I intended to leave, putting as many miles as possible between us so that he could not find us. The pastor sat in silence and complete sympathy, but did not encourage me in any way. I asked if he knew of a children's home headed by the church, that might let us live and me work there, and help other children without parents, a possible solution to getting out of my situation. He discouraged me by saying it was a big frightening world out there, and he would not advise any woman to try to tackle it alone with four children. I thanked him for his time, and walked out more determined than ever to go. I realized I had to call the shots alone and make my own way.

Having no luck at the church, my next move was to ask Mrs. L if the children and I could ride with them to Kansas City; telling her that Columbia, Missouri would be our destination. If we could ride to Kansas City, we would take the bus to Columbia. She confided in her husband; he agreed to this. Knowing my income would be limited, I could not leave Red until the girls were all of school age in order to avoid babysitting fees. Lisa, my youngest, was now in the first grade.

Since Red sometimes helped the girls get ready for school, selection of clothing we could carry had to be discreet. Getting the clothes past him, I knew, would be a challenge. Where to put the clothes we would carry?

Mrs. N was the answer. Upon asking if we could stash them in her closet until time to flee, she suggested her son's closet. He was away at college, and no one ever opened it. She didn't want her husband to know about her help to us, from fear of Red attacking them in some way.

I had to plan every move carefully so as not to endanger anyone.

The clothes were transferred to her house each afternoon during the time Red came to get me after work. From the time he left the house until he returned with me, the girls put the selected garments in big brown grocery bags and put them in Mrs. N's closet. This had to be done quickly, in order to assure that they would be back home by the time we arrived. They made sure Lisa, the youngest, was occupied with something, because she would not understand and could possibly let something slip to Red.

Friday, Labor Day weekend, was to be D-Day (Deliverance Day). As was usual, Red picked me up at lunchtime to take me to the bank and deposit my paycheck. The amount was about $70. That week, I took an old bank receipt from a previous deposit, carefully erased the date, enough to insert the D-Day date. On close examination, I determined that it would have to do, just in case he would ask to see what I had deposited.

As usual, I went alone into the bank. Inside, I cashed the check instead of depositing it. The money was all that I would have for our escape. My insides were churning from nervousness, as he drove me back to work.

On the way, I asked to be dropped off at the sidewalk telephone booth to call Mother Nola in Nashville to report that we were fine; something usually done by me every few weeks.

At this time, he waited in the truck, thinking it was my routine call. Instead, it was to tell her we were leaving him, not to fear that he had done away with us, and that as soon as we were in Columbia, Missouri, I would call her.

She was cautioned to tell no one of my plans except my brother, Buster; and no matter how Red pleaded with them, they were to disavow knowing where we were or if we were alive. If they told him anything, this could possibly mean disaster for the children and me.

I also asked her to be sure that my other siblings knew I was all right. If contacted by him in any way, they were to tell him they knew nothing and that they had not heard from me. Better still, to pretend they had not heard from me in weeks and did not know my whereabouts.

The previous day, Mrs. N had carried the brown grocery bags with our clothes inside over to Mrs. L's house. They were in place. We agreed to rendezvous at ten p.m. at the small shopping center a few blocks away. It would be closed by then. We would be hiding in the dark behind pillars, and they were to flash their lights twice and let us know we could come out when they entered the center.

It was now Friday night, supper was over; we sat down to television. Fortunately, he stayed home, choosing to have a few beers at home that night. This I hoped and prayed would happen.

Soon, he said he was going to bed. As he hesitated in his chair, I looked at his profile, wondering if and somehow feeling that this would be the last time we would see him. Many times, I sat on the side of the bed when I came in to wake him for breakfast. The day before, I repeated that which I had said many times before, "Look into my eyes, Red! Look deep! I have told you over the years that I would leave you if you did not change. The time has come; I intend to keep my word." Then he pulled me down to him, passionately kissed me, and said, "No, you won't. You love Daddy (what the children called him) too much. You wouldn't do that to me." He then flashed his charming smile, assuring himself that this would never be. I went on to say that the marriage license had been nothing but a title of ownership to him, not one of equality, love, patience, kindness, partnership and promises kept. My heart ached as I examined his face and kissed him goodnight. He went back to our bedroom. Later, I listened outside his door to be sure he was asleep.

I hastily wrote him a note saying that we were going away for the weekend for me to think a bit. That if we stayed longer, it would be because I was waiting for assurance that he wanted us back. This could be accomplished by changing his ways. The note was a deliberate attempt to keep him from calling the police and highway patrol to be on the lookout for us. I felt sure he would believe we were still in town when he read it. By the time the weekend was over, however, we would be in another state.

My fears were increased by the memory of what affected my life early in our marriage when Red's brother, Charles, paid a visit to us in Shreveport. He was cordial and the visit was only a few hours, but it brought back memories I struggled to forget. They were not "made for good conversation," for sure. (My heart went out to the relatives affected who led upright, God-fearing lives filled with peace and integrity.)

In the past Charles, his wife, and her parents traveled about from state to state cleaning house (roof) gutters. When they were not working, it was said they were all usually inebriated. During one such vacation at home, Milly, his wife, and he got into a fight. He hit her many times. Then she staggered through the front door and down the steps, the walkway, and collapsed on the steps to the sidewalk. She died shortly after. Because he had beaten her so, he was arrested and charged with murder.

The family didn't have any monies for the legal expenses to help him, so they looked to Red and me for help, promising to repay us after the trial. Although I didn't want to be involved, after Red's pleading for his "brother's life," I succumbed and gave them the money. (Needless to say, I was never repaid any portion of it. That was not important. The crucial matter was what had been done and all should learn from it—those with sense, just plain, every day common sense.) I thought— what a waste—two handsome people wasting their lives drinking and heading down a dead end street, never to return—ever. They would not listen to anyone else with any degree of wisdom.

I did not want to be involved and could tell from Red's comments that I wouldn't be missed, anyway. I was "too straight and religious"... or something to that effect. However, shortly after the trial started he surprised me by a mind change. He began to ask me to please make an appearance at the trial. My answer was always negative. He came back with, "But he is my brother, and I care about what happens to him." I relented and went along, planning to be there only for one visit. While moving about with Red, Charles' lawyer met me and asked if I would sit at the table with him and Charles. He added that I could answer questions he had during the trial. This was certainly a new kind of experience for me.

During the trial, I heard the coroner say that she was severely beaten; however, a final blow to the head caused her death. That next day as I mixed with some of the groups of conversations going on, I overheard a lady tell two others that as she passed the house walking to work, she saw Milly fall down and hit her head on one of the small concrete corner posts at the bottom of the two steps going onto the sidewalk. I could have been anywhere but there at that time, and marveled at my "break." After inquiring about her identity, I immediately relayed this information to the lawyer, assuring that he would see that she did not leave and have her take the stand and say what she saw. This proved to be the key that shifted the tone of conviction. I asked his lawyer if I could be excused from the rest of the trial and, relieved, hurried home. Red and family were so appreciative but he soon returned to his old ways.

CHAPTER 10

At work I left the boss my letter of resignation, explaining to my fellow workers that my marriage had become unbearable, and I was leaving my husband. It was one topic I never discussed at work and, as far as I knew, this was new to them. On all my work, I left notes explaining what had been done and what needed to be done. They were very clear. I tried not to leave any phase of my work undone and unexplained, so as to make my successor's job easy. I apologized for having to leave so abruptly and told the boss I feared my husband, so that he would not think badly of me for leaving my job without prior notice. Fear of leakage of my intentions was my motive for leaving this way.

Lisa was sitting in front of the TV as I hastily got the car keys and my purse. Quietly I said, "Let's go, Lisa! We're going to drive over to the ice cream store and get an ice cream cone."

We hurried out to the car parked at the curb. I had no driver's license and could hardly drive a car, because he always chose to keep and drive the car. As this one was automatic, I finally got it started. The ignition dragged, and I feared he might hear. The windows of the house were open. It was an old car, and I did not realize the handbrake was on the entire time I drove. The brakes were not so good, so he always put the handbrake on when he stopped. In my panicked state of mind, I forgot to release it. It seemed somewhat difficult to drive. Each block, I prayed for it not to break down on us until we could get away. It did not occur to me until later about the handbrake.

When we arrived, I parked the car on the shopping center lot, leaving it unlocked (as usual), with a leaflet of his on the car seat. It was a handout advertising that he was available for cleaning gutters on housetops. This way, I knew someone would see the ad, call the phone number and tell him where to find his car. It was in an open conspicuous place.

We hid behind some wide pillars at the shopping center. It was deserted and dim, much to our advantage. The time was nearing for Mr. and Mrs. L to pick us up. My heart seemed to stop as a couple of cars drove through. The girls cooperated with me. They were warned to stay hidden, so that we could not be seen by any passersby. Lisa did not comprehend what we were doing, but she complied.

At the appointed time a car drove in, blinking its lights off and on. Our escape was here; they had not backed out on us. What a burdensome undertaking for these wonderful people, asking them to encumber their lives with us by helping us now and being silent thereafter.

We hurried into the back seat of the car, after having thrown last-minute items into the trunk that held the brown grocery bags. Off we sped, with me always looking away from light that shown into the car from any source. Relaxing was out of the question until we, at least, could cross the state line.

"We have discussed it, and we cannot go into Kansas City and allow you to take the bus over to Columbia. It is too long a ride, and we want to make sure you are in a hotel before we will leave you alone," Mrs. L said to me as we drove along. This was music to my ears, but I still objected to this inconvenience to them. She said it was no trouble, that they had the entire weekend off.

We spent the night at an inexpensive inn just inside Missouri. This meant my $70 fund was shrinking, hastened, too, by the breakfast we had to buy.

In Columbia we stopped at the Daniel Boone Hotel, getting the last room that they had, as students and parents were in town for college to begin at the University of Missouri for the fall. Many new freshmen were among them, causing the shortage of rooms.

The girls and I crowded into one room, but we were finally free. There was no money to give the L's for our transportation to get us to Missouri, so Teresa's portable record player that she loved was offered in hopes they would give it to a grandchild or relative. Against their strong objection, they took it. To me, it was a meager token of repayment and appreciation. (To Teresa, it was part of her life being given away. This was a revelation of how dearly teens clung to their possessions. I promised her another when a job was obtained.) Our benefactors left for Kansas City.

We chose the cheapest dinner items the hotel offered, so that my funds would not sink too much lower. Of course, the meal was charged to our bill. On returning to the room, the telephone Yellow Pages were perused for a Presbyterian Church. The First Presbyterian Church was just up the street from the hotel.

The next morning was Sunday, and I rose early to phone the pastor's home. "Dr. McMullen, may I please see you today? This is an emergency, and I am in need."

He asked the matter of the plight and I explained that I had four children, fleeing from my husband, and could I see him today at some time?

Between the early-morning sermon and the late-morning service in the sanctuary, he agreed to meet me in the church.

Leaving the children in the room with strict orders to be quiet and not leave the room until I returned, I walked up the street to the church. Dr. McMullen met me and gestured me to a pew. There we sat, as I tearfully told of my flight and my desire to start over again in Columbia. I needed shelter, food and references for me to get a job. He agreed to help me. Because of my pride, I explained that help would only be needed for a couple of months, just enough to get me started.

Dr. McMullen said that two ladies from the church would call on me from a Widows Group (overseers of a fund for widows, but he said I seemed to fit into that category—somewhat). He prayed with me, and I departed.

Later at the Daniel Boone, the phone rang. It was Dr. McMullen. "One of the members of the church owns the hotel you are in. He said there would be no charge for room or food, and that you could stay as long as you need." Was it coincidence that we should choose the hotel owned by a member of the church, and only one vacant room when we arrived? My prayers of gratitude went up.

In the afternoon, two ladies came by and told me to find a place to rent. They would pay for it and bring me some dishes, pots, pans, sheets and pillows, an iron, as well as coupons from the widow's fund for the rent, groceries, and taxi transportation for me to get a job. I was overwhelmed with gratitude and asked that they not tell others that we were so in need.

My pride was wounded. Having to ask for help embarrassed me.

Later, someone wisely rebuked me by saying (and I shall never forget), "Pride is a form of snobbery. If you need help and you don't ask for it, or won't accept someone's gift of love, you are a snob." How wise and profound that became to me.

The church office was offered to me, so that I could call from there for job possibilities.

Within the week, I rented a furnished trailer. It was the only vacancy in the newspaper listings. The onslaught of students took every place available. It was a bad time to seek rental units.

My first job application was to a well-known insurance company. After submitting my application and qualifications, I noticed I was the only one not taking the typing test. Stunned that my return was requested for the next day, and thinking that I was in desperate need of a job "yesterday," I reluctantly left there, bewildered and with questions swimming in my head.

The next day on returning, I was shown into an executive's office. He said, "We apologize for the inconvenience of asking that you return today. However, we felt you were overqualified for our starting jobs and, since I'm on the board of the hospital, would you consider being the Administrator's secretary?" This was joyful news to me. I stammered that I would be delighted to take it.

Dr. McMullen said that he had checked out the references I had given him. The last job reference was a member of the CIA at one time, so I knew that he could keep a secret. The other was a professor at Vanderbilt who said, "We cried when she left us." This particular reply pleased and touched me.

In our hurry to get away, the children's report cards/transfer cards were left on the window sill behind the curtains of my bedroom. Somehow, the teachers believed me when I enrolled them, so they went into the appropriate grades with no problem. Another blessing.

The trailer was furnished with two big beds. Three of the girl slept together, and one with me. Their bed filled up their room, when it was brought down from the wall for sleeping at night. Our home was sparsely furnished, but it was FREEDOM.

The ladies from church brought us a small radio. The plastic covering was chipped and broken, the wire spliced, but it gave us music. The television had faded pictures on it, but we could watch the shadows and listen to the dialogue. No problem; this was FREEDOM.

As the children played outside that weekend, I went from trailer to trailer in the park, asking if anyone drove by the hospital on the way to work. I explained that I was looking for a ride to and from work and would pay for the privilege. Someone pointed out the home of a medical student nearby. His wife was the secretary of a Baptist Church. She said that she would be happy to let me ride with her. Her husband attended the University and drove alone. She drove her own car and would pick me up in the mornings at my trailer door, drop me off, then pick me up after work for our ride home. On food shopping days, I walked to the grocery after work, and took a taxi home. On laundry days, she let me put my baskets into her car on the way to work. After work, she dropped the baskets and me off. After doing the laundry, I took a taxi home. When money ran out before payday, it was necessary to launder some things in the bathroom and dry them inside the trailer via inside clothesline.

The girls were adjusting at school. My job was challenging, and my coworkers were all enjoyable and helpful.

On Sunday mornings, the girls and I went to church. We took a taxi in, worshiped, and then walked up a few blocks to the hospital. There, I used employee discount coupons for lunch. So, one day a week, we were treated to a splendid cafeteria lunch. We were grateful. It was freedom at last.

The budget was tight. My earnings had to go a long way. The girls remember me counting the cookies, wrapping and putting them in the cabinet, daring anyone to touch them. They were for lunch and were put in their brown bags with a sandwich and the occasional piece of fruit. There was lunch money for the older girls that I put aside and meted out daily. Free lunch at school was not available.

Once my morning cup of coffee was made, if there was left over, it was poured into a cup for the next day. The pot was a 4 cup variety with a base that could easily catch on the eye of the gas unit and tilt over. It had to be exactly placed on the stove or coffee could be wasted when it perked. The coffee that was bought had to be rationed carefully.

The tank of gas for cooking seemed to empty quickly. It seemed time flew to replenish the heating tank also. Food was scarce, but I managed to get a dinner together each evening, planned to be as good and nourishing as possible.

The grocery day was happily anticipated by us all. It meant a carton of eight colas (the carton always displayed the extra two colas for the price of six—double colas). Along with the carton was the treat of pimento cheese in a dairy tin, scooped out with luscious potato chips. We ate until they were all gone. It did not seem a crumb was left over nor a sip of cola left. It would be two weeks until my payday and "dessert" again.

Then there were utilities, my ride, coins for the laundry, a tip for the taxi, monthly rent, school supplies that were or were not anticipated, and the milkman.

"What I need is a sugar daddy," I blurted out one wintry night as I carefully peeled the counted potatoes I'd planned to cook for dinner. This came out as a result of my frustration at having to be so precise about everything.

"Mama, what's a sugar daddy?" Susan asked. I did not notice that she was in earshot.

Embarrassed and ashamed, I quickly said, "That is someone who brings candy to all of us, someone who likes to give candy to others," I mumbled something I thought was coherent to satisfy her innocent mind. There was no other response; apparently my explanation was sufficient.

One fellow employee who had gone to work across the street in the medical building for private doctors often came into the office to chat for a moment. We soon became good friends.

She had two sons during her now failed marriage. They were in their late teens. In addition to her daily job, she took dictation home with her and transcribed it in order to supplement her salary. She was the fastest typist I had ever encountered. Her name was Nita. The oldest son was going to college and working, too. The youngest planned to also go to college; another expense she would have in the near future.

One day, the Vice Chief of Staff at the hospital came into my office. He greeted me and sat down opposite me, asking when my boss would return. Small talk ensued, then he said with a slight smile on his face, "Do you have a sister like you who would like to work in my office?"

This was a new-to-me hiring approach, I thought. Apparently it was not kosher here at the hospital to openly take an employee away from her present job.

When Nita came by, the doctor's quick but right to the point conversation was mentioned to her. She urged me to go talk to him. More money, medicine for the children and me, and a yearly bonus could be possible.

When contacted, the doctor suggested my visit be soon. His partner also came by and visited me briefly, suggesting a move for "someone" would be a good idea.

Within a couple of weeks, my resignation was given. It was not easy to do, but necessary. I went in as receptionist and, within a few months, became the office manager.

After a few weeks, Dr. G learned that I had no car. He mentioned that real estate was his other pursuit and he would look around to purchase a house he could rent to me within walking distance. Soon this materialized, and my family became occupants in a quiet, comfortable neighborhood.

Since I did the bookkeeping, I could take my rent out in two halves each month, not causing a hardship on my budget. My few pieces of furniture were bought at auction and flea markets. Dr. G loaned us a refrigerator. We were comfortable. At Christmas time, the two doctors surprised me with a washing machine as my bonus. The late night trips to the laundromat became history. I was so grateful for my gift. (My "dryer" was still the clothesline strung up in the basement.)

Dr. G's brother provided us with free emergency dental care. When other doctors had to be seen by the children or me, there was never a bill received by us.

Every time someone hesitated at my office door on my previous job or in the reception room at my new job, my heart skipped a beat from fear that we had been found. Many times, while I was still at the hospital, it was Dr. McMullen from the church. When he caught my attention, he would smile, throw his hands upward and shake his head, as if in disbelief.

"When you told me your story, I thought you were the bravest woman I ever knew, or it was the best con story I had ever heard." Dr McMullen had been born in

China to an American missionary, who became president of a university there.

The girls were growing up fast, physically. The terrible teens were there for two of them; the other two would emulate them or ask why their sisters got more than they did. The friction began to show.

One morning Robin stayed home from school because she was ill. This proved to be her first day of moving into young womanhood. My work schedule was to go in late to the office and stay late to be sure that all information was available on the patients coming in the next morning. For example: lab reports and any other pertinent information concerning the patient.

As I readied myself for work, in conversation with Robin, I related a strange dream of the previous night.

"Last night I dreamed I woke up late in the morning; apparently you girls were all gone to school. I jumped up and examined the alarm clock on the dresser; nothing else was there. The clock had stopped at 15 minutes of the hour. I ran to the telephone to get the correct time, wondering how late I was for work. I dialed the time information. It was not the clear voice of the lady giving correct time and a brief advertisement, but of a man who was so inebriated his voice sounded like an old-time record player that was dragging, and the player needed to be rewound. I was so exasperated that I could not get the correct time. How late for work was I?"

Within 30 minutes after describing the dream, the phone rang. It was Mother Nola from Nashville, saying she had bad news. In that instant, all sorts of tragic possibilities ran through my mind.

"Clara, someone called from Louisiana a few minutes ago. Raymond (Red) was killed in a car wreck last night." Her voice sounded weary.

Before I lost my composure, I added, "Mother Nola, please call them back and make sure it was not someone else, a mistaken identity. I'll wait here at the phone. Please!"

Within half an hour the phone rang again and she confirmed the first call. He was physically described, and it was added that he had a Civitan medal around his neck. It was surely he, because Red never went without my medal around his neck. It bore my name and the date on it. This last call negated the idea that this was a ruse to get me out of hiding.

How horrible for him to die, especially like this. My emotions caused me to panic, to cry uncontrollably. It frightened Robin, but she proved to be the stronger one here.

"Mom, get hold of yourself! You didn't cause this." She tried her best to console me. Then she called the schools and asked that her sisters be sent home.

Not wishing to deal with the varied emotions of those who did or did not know about our past stormy marriage, I chose not to go home for the funeral. The chief reason, however, was that there were no funds to get me home, just as with Papa and my sister, Donie. He was so damaged, it was a closed casket, I was later to learn.

When we received his death certificate, it shocked me to find that he had died instantly, exactly 15 minutes of the hour, the time the clock had stopped in my dream. Coincidence? (The dream had been related to Robin, at least half an hour before the first call came in from Mother Nola.)

After getting Nita and others to mind the girls, I took a bus (my vacation week) to Springfield, Missouri and took a course with a company that approached me to sell securities. They paid my expenses, hoping that I would join their firm. The week was exhausting. In order to study, I rose early and went to bed late. Classes were all day, every day. Then I went to the university and took one exam, passed it, and went to the Capitol building for the second and passed it. I now had a license to sell securities. Since there was no fear in returning to Nashville, this could be an option for a new career. I had passed my federal exam, but would have to pass the state exam also in the state where I chose to work.

The next year, my plans were finalized and we returned home to Nashville, at last. In Nashville, my nephew, Gene, drove me around to look at some half-dozen furnished apartments he had selected for me to see. I chose one within walking distance of my work. (The bus was for bad weather days.) My job was back at Vanderbilt, but now in the medical school as secretary for Dr. M, professor of surgery and surgical pathology.

The oldest girls were into the hippie movement, and had strong opinions about their futures. Following behind were the younger two, just as independent, but more subdued and obedient. My combats were many. They were definitely four individuals with separate outlooks. They all had good hearts, but they wanted to spread their wings, and Mom was too tame. One called me neither male nor female, but neuter, because I didn't date and "have fun like the other mothers they knew." Only with God's help, did we survive those additional tumultuous years.

Robin married young. She chose a Vietnam veteran who had Hodgkin's disease. It did no good to tell her that he only had a short time to live. She was determined to keep him alive, no matter what it took. She accompanied and nursed him through the first chemotherapy ever offered here (experimental treatments).

My first car was a Plymouth obtained for $600 from a coworker at Vanderbilt. Her family was leaving the state and she planned to co-share their other car with her husband.

CHAPTER 11

Our abode was a first floor apartment. Directly above us were three law students who made lots of noise, especially when they had a party. The celebrations seemed to be late and often and, sometimes, the "stomping" shook our overhead chandelier.

On one particular day, it was about two a.m. and, of course, we had retired several hours before and were fast asleep.

Suddenly jolted awake by a pounding noise that seemed to come from the sliding glass doors that led to the balcony from my living room, I got up, put on my house shoes and night robe to find out from where the noise came. I walked down the hall's short distance from my bedroom and went to the door to be sure it was still locked. Then I walked over to the sliding glass doors and I pulled the drapes aside but saw nothing.

"Must be one of the guys upstairs trying to get in over his balcony rail and found the sliding doors locked," I muttered sleepily as I returned to bed.

After returning to sleep, I was awakened again by this same pounding. Up for the second time, I again went to the sliding door and saw nothing. By this time, sleepily irritated, since they apparently were not on my balcony that I could see, I determined to go back to bed and ignore the noise. There was a third time, and I rolled over on my side and ignored it.

About five a.m., I arose and called Robin to get ready for school. She would fix her own cereal and juice so that I could sleep an extra hour. Her habit was to hurriedly dress and then go to the small dining room off the kitchen and living room and breakfast there.

After I was relaxed and asleep, she shook me and whispered with fear in her voice, "Mom, there's a man in our living room."

I didn't move or open my eyes. "Robin, this is no time to be joking; I want my extra sleep."

(My four daughters were always saying if a man ever came into our house, they would put him in the closet and lock the door so he couldn't get away from them. That was the only way, they concluded, that I would ever get a man.)

"Mom, I'm not joking. There is a man on our couch in the living room. Please come see for yourself! Honest!" She had fright in her voice. She convinced me.

Again, I hurried into my shoes and robe and, together, we crept down the hall. The lamp table was next to the couch. So we peered around the lamp and the man was slumped at our end, sleeping soundly, and reeking of liquor.

I hastily whispered, "Get your sisters up and get next to the front door, because he might wake up and get violent. I've never seen him before." Robin quickly got her sleepy sisters up, and it didn't take long for the situation to frighten them—a stranger in the living room.

After they gathered at the door, I instructed them to stay there while I hurried to the manager's apartment to call the police. We were exceptionally quiet, whispering that if he should arouse, they were to flee the apartment.

The manager immediately answered my impatient knock on her door. I told her there was a man in our apartment and he was drunk. "Do you know him?" she asked. I thought this was a silly question and mentally said, "Why would I be here if I did?"

"Never saw him before in my life. Apparently he hammered on my door until he got it open, and went to sleep on my couch. I heard the pounding, as if with a big rock, but thought it was a student from upstairs and finally went to bed and ignored it."

With that explanation, she hurried to the phone and called the police. Within a very short time after my arrival back inside the apartment, the police arrived.

They immediately went to him, pulling him up to a standing position and began a series of questions. His legs seem to buckle under him as they held him up.

"Where do you think you are?" One demanded loudly. "I'm in my dad's house." He answered with slurred speech. "Where is that?" He fired another question. "In Nashville, Indiana." The intruder answered as he opened his eyes slightly. He tottered as he tried to regain some balance. "Let's go downtown!" The officer ordered as they held him up to escort him away.

The whole episode had exhausted me, so I phoned in and took the day off from work... something I seldom did.

The next day an MP phoned and identified himself to me. He also gave the name of the young man that had broken into our apartment. On talking further, I learned that he was a soldier and had served in Vietnam. This was his first trip home. Apparently he got off the bus in the wrong town and state, possibly took a taxi only to be let out at the wrong place again.

The Military Police asked if I would come to the station and press charges. My answer was no way. He had served his country well and to please let him go... that he had not hurt us in any way, did not take anything from us... to tell him I wished him well. Please don't punish him in the slightest way!!! I never heard from them again and I assumed/hoped all went well for the young man.

In that same apartment one Saturday morning, I told my daughters that I planned to phone an old school friend who had been a neighbor. This call was to congratulate him on the enormous success of his daughter singing solo on a very popular national weekly television show.

I told them I had only seen Mr. R a couple of times since school, but upon my return to Nashville saw him daily on a morning show (when I had time to glance toward the TV in my haste to get ready to go to work).

The two times that I could remember seeing him were 1) as I waited in the car for Red in front of the Court House many years ago, and 2) when Red and I rode past the Ernest Tubb (a regular on the Grand Ole Opry) Record Shop. We had double parked in front of the shop waiting to observe the fans and to briefly watch the weekly (Saturday) midnight show that originated from there. As usual, the crowd began to grow, since the Grand Ole Opry had signed off for the night. The Record Shop always broadcast into the night with country music Opry stars as the guests.

I noticed two men approaching our pickup truck. It was Mr. R and Carl Smith (a star at that time). Mr. R was jovial as he introduced me as his girlfriend as he had since we were children (actually it was one-sided—the crush—because I liked Randall; he often gave his girl little gifts)... Mr. R asked if we wanted to come in; he was going to be on the show. I sensed that Red was miffed as he straightened up quickly, only slightly acknowledging the introductions and saying to me, "Let's go!" Without further word he hastily drove us away. I never saw Mr. R again.

That Saturday morning he answered the phone when I called him. I told him I had returned to Nashville and wanted to congratulate him on his success and especially his daughter's. He seemed pleased to hear from me, asking about where I lived in Nashville (the usual mundane polite conversation of a "celebrity," just a little more extensive than to a first-time fan). No matter to me; I did what I thought was appropriate—to verbalize my praise for both of them.

The girls had listened to my part of the conversation and then scattered to do their household duties and prepare for afternoon fun with friends. I, too, began my customary weekend work.

In about half an hour, there was a knock at the door. I opened it, and to my amazement, there stood Mr. R. I must have looked stunned. How could he have arrived so fast when it seemed like I just hung up? An invitation for a visit was certainly not in our conversation. Why was he here? After gaining my composure, I invited him in and introduced him to my four daughters. (They looked as shocked as I.)

We sat at the dining room table, with my daughters taking turns listening to our conversation. This pleased me, because they could verify what was said by both of us. My reputation as a good Mom was always at stake—wanting to be a moral example for them.

We talked about school, the old neighborhood and about my residence in different states. He wanted to know where, because he had inquired over the past few years about my whereabouts, but no one knew.

Each time I excused myself to go to the back part of the apartment, I would always caution the girls not to leave me. As the morning went into the afternoon, they became restless, wanting to assure last minute plans for their anticipated evening.

Not sure of his marital status at one point, I bluntly inquired, "Where does your wife think you are?"

"In Kentucky on business," he replied.

This added to my uneasiness. Most certainly I was happy to spend my Saturday morning conversing with my friend of many years ago, but how would this look to his family and mine? Was I too hasty to imagine too much in this seemingly innocent encounter?

During the very few brief times that one daughter was not with us, he would switch to a very personal note, telling me how much his dad had always wanted us to marry. How happy he would be to know that Mr. R had found me. I cringed at these comments and hastily changed the tone to inquire about his father's health (I was always very fond of his parents and found this to be a diversion from talking about us).

In the late afternoon, he suggested that we drive across town to our old neighborhood where we grew up as children. In quick conversation with the daughters (one would sit and chat with Mr. R while I was away those few moments), I literally begged for them to decide which one had the least promising/fun evening out so that she could stay with me. Robin volunteered.

To Mr. R, I said that she would have to go along with us, since leaving her alone in the apartment would not be wise. This was stretching the truth somewhat, but it fit the situation. No one could frown on our "visit" if a young teenager was with us at all times. I sighed a breath of relief when we got into the car and Robin sat in the back seat with elbows on the space between us in the front seat—a position where she could hear everything.

We drove all over the area of our yesteryears, reminiscing as we passed familiar landmarks—especially our grammar school where he entered on the (Madison Street) Boys side and I the (Jefferson Street) Girls side. The engraving in the concrete was still there. Robin seemed to be enjoying the ride, especially since we were in such an expensive automobile.

By this time, he suggested dinner somewhere, to which I objected. Then he stopped at a liquor store and brought out a bottle of champagne (to "celebrate our reunion," Mr. R said). Then we drove back to our apartment.

There were no champagne glasses in my kitchen, so I brought out two of my best glasses (two that matched, that were not plastic). He started to pour mine, "Let's celebrate our reunion!"

"Thank you, but no. I'm a teetotaler." I smiled, not wanting to be rude.

Mr. R filled his glass, held it up as if to toast me and began to drink. It was growing late, nearing 9 p.m. Very soon the girls would be coming home from the movies and visiting their friends. He didn't seem to be anxious at all. Soon, he moved to the couch, sans glass, and sat down comfortably as if to stay. I had envisioned when I left the apartment with him that he would tire of Robin tagging along and let us out of the car when we returned and bid us farewell. But no, he soon lay his head on the back of the couch and went fast asleep.

Sometimes, the girls would bring their friends home with them for a few minutes along with a parent or two. A man asleep on my couch? What would they think? That I was now a "hussy"? That I hid behind a cloak of deception? Ah, then their children would not be allowed to spend such lengthy hours visiting with my family. All kinds of thoughts went through my head. Perhaps I was making a "mountain out of a molehill," as my mother used to say.

Shortly, Susan came home, walking in with one of her best friends. They jolted to a stop when they spied the man asleep on our couch. Before I could explain, Susan's friend Beth said, "I know him. His son dates my sister." These were words I did not want to hear.

Hastily, I explained that he was an old friend from our days as children, and he had paid me a visit to talk about old times—since we had not seen each other in many years. "He got comfortable or bored and went to sleep," I stammered. (Mentally I was praying that Beth would accept this explanation; because her mother, too, had attended high school with me, and I expected her to tell Jane about this.)

Soon, Mr. R awoke, gave me a quick hug (under Robin's watchful eye), explaining he'd better get home and that he enjoyed the day very much. To my relief, nothing more.

Sunday went by without "incident." However, my phone rang very early as I dressed for work on Monday morning. It was he. "Clara, will you please go to breakfast with me?" Mr. R asked. I replied that I couldn't, thanked him and hurried back to my readying for work. The next morning he phoned and my answer was the same. For the next three days, one of the girls answered to say that I had already gone to work.

On Saturday about lo a.m., the phone rang and it was Mr. R again. He talked more rapidly than usual. "My wife is on the other line. Will you explain that I was there last Saturday, that we are grammar school friends, nothing more? That it's been more than ten years since I saw you last—if not more." He went on to say that his son's girlfriend had told her that he was asleep in my living room. The dialogue with his wife was both apologetic and gracious, and I apologized that his visit had caused her distress. I thanked him for his visit and asked that he always bring her along on any future visits. Of course, there were none.

CHAPTER 12

My boss, Dr. Mac, retired. He gave up surgery, but went back to Vanderbilt to see patients. He chose to work in the laboratory of a local community hospital in Madison (an area of Nashville). I went along with him on his limited retirement. The children and I moved to that area of town so that I could be near work again.

I became acquainted with Margit at my new apartment. We met a couple of days after she came to Nashville. Her family moved into the apartment opposite us. Our entrances faced each other in the connecting hallway, her door being just a few feet away.

When their furniture arrived from Pennsylvania, there was no one to help her move into the apartment. Teresa was home that day and asked Margit if she needed help. They became fast friends, while moving her in all that day.

When I came home from work, Teresa said, "Mom, I've been helping the new lady move in. She is so interesting.

They are in Nashville to open a smorgasbord restaurant. She was born in Czechoslovakia. Her husband will be the cook, and she calls him 'Pop'... they have three boys and one girl. Right now all but the oldest boy, Bob, are remodeling a house on a hill on Dickerson Pike, and they hope to open up soon. Bob is in college. She was alone trying to move all that stuff in." Teresa was filled with excitement as she talked on and on that evening.

Another family from Pennsylvania had previously moved into our apartment complex. They were partners in this business, and had selected the restaurant site. Later, we met them, too. Both families worked on the retaurant for weeks. It was called the Country House.

This was my first information about Margit who would become my loyal friend, no matter what the circumstances for us all.

The girls worked for her at the Country House, by washing dishes after school, and then rushing home to dress to waitress for the evening. They also worked in the yard helping with the planting and watering of flowers. They hosed down the plastic runners for the floors, and replenished the salad bar. (They asked her to employ them so they could help Mama pay the bills.)

One now-amusing incident was a crowded Mother's Day. The restaurant was packed. People were outside waiting to get in. Lisa was rushing to get desserts to a table of many and did not set the filled tray securely on the table. It tipped over and desserts crashed to the floor. She was barely 14, and this was just too much stress. She threw her hands up, ran to the pantry, babbling, "I quit," and burst into tears. Susan, the cool-headed one, cleaned up the mess with the help of the busboys, and then rushed to find Lisa. She coaxed her back to her station saying, "It's no problem. It happens to everyone at some time."

That same day I had delivered the girls by car for work before the doors opened for business. Pop asked me to go to the nearest supermarket and get as many rolls as possible, which I did. I was in a very casual pants suit and wanted to stay out of the dining rooms. The female help were all in long, quaint, print dresses. When I returned, he asked me to fill the bread warmer at the main food line, then go to the other hot foods line in the outer side dining room, and also fill that one. By the time the second was filled, the first was empty, and this went on until one hour before closing.

Susan was married on the lawn of the Country House. Her husband, Gary, was a career military man. (She would turn 17 the following month.)

Margit furnished the location and the reception, a neighbor of ours who attended Margit's church made the formal white dress for me—no charge—I furnished the material. Another church neighbor chipped in by doing errands for us. The partner at the Country House Smorgasbord was a part-time minister and performed the ceremony. No charge. It was a beautiful and memorable affair that cost me very little.

The bride was stunning, and the groom was handsome and charming. The next year, my first grandchild was born in Germany, near Gary's military base. They named her Nancy.

After a time, I approached an old school friend about selling real estate. Prior to this, my insurance examination was passed, and license secured. However, I wanted to get into real estate. I studied for the exam and passed it. With real estate license in hand, I began a new career. Why so many job changes? I was always in the pursuit of more income so that my children could have a better living.

Because my Plymouth had no air conditioning, my broker suggested selling me one of his cars that had this luxury (a must for prospective customers).

My dear neighbor told me they were looking for a location to open a new restaurant of their own in order to sever the ties with their partner. Upon approaching my broker with a description of Margit's need, he could suggest only one house offered for sale. It belonged to a schoolteacher, but was not zoned commercial.

I drove to the house, approaching it from different directions, and finally went into the driveway, knowing I couldn't go inside just yet. But what I saw from the outside seemed excellent. Bingo! This was perfect.

At the office, I assured my broker that she would buy. He put a sizable amount of money down on the house to discourage any other potential buyer. Then he approached a previous prospective buyer. His name was Charlie.

He and my broker visited the Country House as customers, observed the operation and came out satisfied.

If I could not secure a loan for her to buy the house herself, then Charlie could step in, buy it, and lease it to her.

After much persuasion, I finally got her and Pop on contract to buy the house. Interest rates were up, and lending was down. After being turned down by several lenders, which was not unusual for anyone else buying at that time, the last place offered us a loan for three years. It was a balloon note. The company offered us reasonable monthly payments for three years, with the balance being due at that time. She refused the loan.

Charlie then bought the house and offered a lease with the assurance that he would make whatever changes that would have to be made to make it the restaurant she wanted, such as adding dining rooms and kitchen. (Before Margit came along, my broker had tried to sell Charlie the corner, but he was never interested. Now he was excited about this new challenge.) I breathed a sigh of relief over the outcome, because my broker would have lost his earnest money if one of them had backed out. By now, I had been working on this deal for several months.

What a close call! Charlie bought the house just three days before our option was up. Another company's agent told me she had a buyer on contract, waiting for our deal to fall through. If it had, my friend would have possibly moved back to Pennsylvania.

Now, we were getting her family a location of their very own.

Huge dining rooms were added, as well as a kitchen and waitress stations. The existing rooms were made into private dining rooms for small groups.

Primarily, used equipment furnished the kitchen; however, some new machines were bought. Margit and I made trips to Pennsylvania to secure furnishings to give it a homey, antique look. Her taste in decorating was excellent.

At first she was fearful of this whole venture, but I told her, "Pop can do the cooking and food buying, you do the decorating and furnishing, I'll be the 'yes person' and take care of the payroll and finances. No problem." Sure enough, it took off. The restaurant opened and business was excellent from the beginning.

I put my real estate selling on hold for a time and worked at the restaurant. Teresa and Lisa worked there after school most days. Teresa entered the new community college, commuting every day.

When the Country Music Association held its televised awards show, Margit invited the participants from all the foreign country bands to be her guests. They all came. Lisa waited on the tables, paying special attention to the Czech band members. She was introduced to André. During his short stay, she dated him. They stayed in close touch. On his next trip in, they were engaged to be married. Lisa had started community college by then, but dropped out to go to Germany to visit Susan. Soon, she was in Prague, Czechoslovakia to marry André. His father made them an apartment in their home, by remodeling the basement. The parents occupied the first floor, and a relative occupied the second.

André was the only child of his parents. They worked in government jobs. The father had been born into an apparently wealthy family, but the real estate was taken from them by the Communist government to be distributed. André's father was an accomplished artist, whose paintings were to have been in a Paris exhibit. But when Prague was occupied, the Paris showing was canceled, and life as it once was drastically changed.

André's parents had urged him to pursue a musical career. They firmly believed that his musical ability would keep him alive in the event that he was placed in a concentration camp; that his chances for survival would be greater. He pursued the violin, as well as other instruments. At age 11, he had been a guest violinist with the Prague Symphony.

Lisa and he were married in Prague.

In my calls to her, she said the basement apartment was lovely and quite comfortable. She was happy to be there with him, and she bubbled with interesting and abundant stories by mail and phone. His parents adored her, and she them. Once she made them American hamburgers. They proved to be so large that Father had to sacrifice his impeccable European good manners to open his mouth wide enough to consume it. This was quite funny to her. Then Father took her to get a Christmas tree. She selected the fullest one and left him in the yard to trim it. When he brought it in , she did not dare show anything but appreciation, but she was horrified. The tree looked like the limbless one in the well-known American comic strip. However, she thanked him profusely and proceeded to decorate it.

André traveled with the band quite often into surrounding countries. Most were Communist. Once Lisa went into Poland to be with him, to see his performance, and she was kept at the Polish border for questioning for several hours. She was too naïve and young to be frightened. He chose to play with a country band because it meant more money, and he was able to travel broadly, though always in restricted boundaries under strict rules.

My health began to decline. The doctor said that I needed an operation on the carotid artery. Arteriograms showed my neck's right side to be normal, but the left one was blocked. I knew enough to know that was indeed bad news. My vision began to play tricks on me. I was seeing only parts of people and objects. This had been occurring several times a day.

After surgery and a long rest that could not be afforded, the thought came to me that the family could be given jobs with my supervision if we, too, opened a smorgasbord. Margit could not afford to hire us all, so this would simplify the situation. However, it would be necessary to select an area of Nashville that would not be in competition to her business. I thought of a house we visited when I showed her possible locations for her business.

I made an appointment with the owner. Bill was running his real estate company out of the house. It was still a home that could be sold for family occupancy, since he had done very little to change any part of it. I walked through again and asked him if anyone had a contract on it. He said he had several people who were interested. The house was in Hendersonville, a suburb of Nashville. It was on the main street.

The tourists were always going by there on the way to visit The House of Cash (museum), homes of country star Johnny Cash, Conway Twitty, and other notables. Excellent location. Bingo!

How was I to get the money, since my balance in the bank was below a hundred dollars? I began to draw on my securities knowledge. My first investor gave me a check for earnest money. On the next Monday morning, I took a contract to Bill. Additional stock would be sold to get me cash for the down payment and closing. A small business loan would be secured for equipment, changes and additions to the existing structure. Trips to city Council meetings would get me zoned commercial and tell me how to comply.

In order to save money, every corner was cut. For example, a student at Vol State College drew the house plans for me as the structure presently stood, inch by inch. From this, copies were made so that I could combine rooms, close closets and make them into waitress stations, and select the kitchen site, add walk-in freezers, dish-washing lines and other needs.

To my ex-broker who had helped me get started in the real estate business and to whom I felt a favor was owed, I gave the job of making the house into a restaurant. He was to remodel the house, add a huge kitchen, hot foods, salad, and dishwashing areas. Teresa and I went to a restaurant exhibit at McCormick Center in Chicago to select equipment and some furnishings. The entire project was consumed with details that seemed to multiply by hundreds daily.

Prior to this, with the help of her sisters, Teresa had visited Prague to meet André's family and to see Lisa. After a few days, she phoned me to get her out of there and get her a flight to Germany to spend the rest of her time with Susan and Gary. She was not happy with the Communist climate, but did love the people. She had become quite outspoken in her recent years, actually going back to the last months we spent with Red; therefore, her "opinions" could get her in trouble, so speed was of the essence in getting her across the border.

A honey of a deal was presented me when I went looking for a residence near the restaurant. It was a home, complete with furniture on a cul-de-sac street. At the end, a house between us, was the historic residence of a friend of President Andrew Jackson. The story I heard was that her father was strict and did not want her to marry. She wanted to elope. Jackson helped his suitor friend to fetch her from the second floor by way of a ladder, thereby, enabling the couple to escape her father.

As we labored to get the restaurant house remodeled and furnishings ordered, we moved into our new home. I gave Robin and Jimmy the master bedroom so that they would have a private bath. Susan moved back to Nashville, and she and Nancy shared a house with Teresa. All four daughters were now nearby. The completion of the restaurant seemed to drag. During this time, Jimmy died, throwing Robin into deep mourning and depression. I remember my first words of encouragement to her were, "This, too, will pass." This was a phrase often used by me, orally and mentally, when there was a crisis. And there had been many. She often said to me that the statement had helped her personally through that loss and many other losses that followed.

Our smorgasbord opened late, causing a financial wedge in my capital. Hopefully, this could be remedied in the near future. It was beautiful, with all hand-picked furnishings, pictures, paintings, and curtains. Each room was graced with a different homey décor, inviting the guests to relax and enjoy good food. There were silk flowers in the vases, live plants hanging in the restrooms, carvings and pictures bought during the foreign travels of the family.

The father of one of the music superstars that frequented our place said his family had to come home to us to get the best meal in the country. These types of compliments were received daily, and our business began to grow by word-of-mouth from satisfied customers.

Daily my routine meant going to each area of the smorgasbord often, to be sure customers were served and that all areas were clean. After inspection by the health watchdogs, they usually stayed and had lunch with us. This was most certainly a compliment. Food tasting was also a chore of mine, to be sure that it was palatable to the mouth and eyes. It was also important to me to treat my employees with the same respect I gave to my own family members. My philosophy was: if they enjoyed their work, they made excellent employees.

The children often said, "Mom, when we enter that front door to work each day, we cease to be your children; we become employees."

I responded "You're right. You must be an example of the right thing to do. Make your time here busy and enjoyable! The family must have the right attitude toward each other, too." Another way of saying, LOVE thy neighbor as thyself.

Lisa and André came from Czechoslovakia soon after we opened the restaurant. Teresa and Susan worked the salads, along with other help. Lisa worked in the hot foods, along with two other cooks. Robin ran the cash register and greeted the guests. André washed dishes.

One day as André labored away, he got a business-like call. To afford him privacy, I left him alone at the telephone and returned after his conversation.

"Mother," he said to me in his heavy accent, "That was Charley Pride."

After my shock that he should be personally calling André, I stammered, "Wait a minute, André! What did he want?"

"He wants me on the airplane to visit him on Friday to talk about money. Charley will be at the airport to take me to his home and to meet the tailor to fit me for my clothes, if I agree to play for him," he added nonchalantly. I followed closely behind him as he headed back to the dish-washing area.

"André, do you know how many musicians in Nashville would love to be in your position right now?"

Lisa appeared and he explained that he had to be away for the weekend, but would fly back late Monday.

When he returned on Monday, he was laden with tapes of Charley's songs. He had been hired, was told to practice by playing his fiddle along with the tapes, and become familiar with each song. He practiced the entire week. This was no sweat for him; his talent showed through. Many times he picked up the guitar and played along with the tape, to be prepared in the event he was needed in that area also. There was no doubt that he was extremely talented.

Gary was stationed near Savannah, Georgia. He came home often, usually on the weekends. It was so good to have them all at home. And we all loved the restaurant.

Many times, my thoughts returned to my school days and the joy of knowing each classmate. The idea came to me to close the doors to customers one evening, and invite out my graduating class of 1946 for a reunion. As verbal invitations were given on the phone, each was asked to contact as many as were remembered so that no one would be overlooked. A small combo of musicians, including a relative of the famous Guy Lombardo (known for New York's New Year's Eve Times Square, Auld Lang Syne—that traditional melody), a female pediatrician who played for fun, along with another equally good entertainer, was hired by me. The combo was excellent, and welcomed heartily by all.

Most of my graduating class showed up, along with their husbands and wives. We had a wonderful time (being young again). The men actually tossed a football down a hall that connected dining rooms. Several times, they barely missed the chandeliers. Other times they sat on the floor instead of using the chairs. My daughters said my guests almost had to be pushed out the door to close the party. Certainly, it was a night to be remembered the rest of our lives.

Several of them later told me that other classes heard of our wonderful time and decided to make a yearly event of 25 graduating classes of our high school. They insisted the idea stemmed from our reunion at my restaurant for the class of 1946. The reunions continue even now.

One day Lisa said, "Mom, do you remember me telling you that when we arrived at Opryland for André to audition with the other foreign entertainers for the awards show that I had to drive him to buy a guitar pick? He left his at home. He was moved to the last audition because of this. Because he was not here with his usual band, he sang, played the guitar for himself, then did 'Orange Blossom Special' on the fiddle. Charley came in shortly before André played and caught his performance.

He started talking to André after he heard him. André, in his broken English, told him he did not understand, so I introduced myself to interpret for him. Charley asked me to send him a demo to Dallas of André singing and playing the instruments. That's the demo you paid for. Remember?" That was a quirk of fate that had completely left my mind. A quirk with a good result. We both chuckled, remembering that André forgot his pick and got a job as the result.

Soon after we opened the restaurant, Robin greeted me with, "Mom, it's time for you to get a good car." The other girls agreed with her. "My van is now paid off from Jimmy's insurance, so there will be no problem with down payment," she added.

Reluctantly, I went along to see what she had in mind. It was the latest model Cadillac—silver and beautiful.

"You must be kidding! Me? In this?" The car would be my third. The first was bought for $600, the second had air conditioning, and now this? I considered it top-of-the-line (from childhood memories of cars seen by me). This would be my first brand new car. Wow!

My objections were many, but Robin overcame them with the argument that it could last me my lifetime with the proper care. She said maintenance would be my only expense in the future. Over my strongest objections, she finally won out.

My new car was silver, Wilma Rudolph's was gold (she was a gold-medal winner for the United States in the Olympics), and Conway Twitty's was dark red (he was a superstar Country Music performer). All of us resided in the Hendersonville area. For me to drive a car just like the ones they drove stunned me. I had not seen another model of this Cadillac in our area, except for the three aforementioned. My gratitude was beyond description. A business of my own, a home of my own, and...—and... and, now a car?

Going into the third year, the business was hit by a rough January. There was snow on ice, layers of it. Customers were not coming out in the bad weather and, if they could make it home from work, they stayed. They did not stop for restaurant food. The mortgage notes, utilities and salaries for key employees went on, though there was no business. The winter and the bills were harsh. What to do? Every day food had to be put on the line, regardless of the number of customers that showed up. To close up until better weather came was erratic and could cause customers to consider us unreliable.

The girls began to be restless. Susan wanted to go to Georgia to be with her husband, Gary. Lisa wanted to live in Dallas to be near André's work base. Teresa had married one of the young men who worked for us, and Gary had convinced them that the army was an excellent future for them.

The bad weather seemed to seal our fate. Only a large sum of money could save us. Additionally, my health was an issue that was brought up by my family. We closed the restaurant.

They went their separate ways, sadly, but clearly by necessity. My heart was broken by the loss of the business and my family going in so many directions. But this was life (the human condition of imperfection and uncertainty). A profound trust in God was needed by me again. My business, my fancy car, and my home were lost. There were no assets left. My bank balance was back to zero again. My heart ached for the stockholders who had believed in me. This, too, affected my health.

Robin, Susan, and I rented a house in Savannah, Georgia. Gary was based nearby. After a few months working for a company in Savannah, my life began to change again.

Lisa wanted me to visit and stay with her for awile in Dallas. To pay my expenses while there, a job was necessary. I found one in real estate, managing apartments. Because Lisa also needed a job, I negotiated a job for me only if they took her, too.

Soon, Teresa phoned that she was pregnant and needed me where she was based in Germany. By that time, Lisa had learned the apartment managing job well with my tutoring, so it was no problem for me to leave Dallas.

Teresa lacked only a few months having a college degree, but could not be an officer, because her husband had not attended college. So, their income was limited because of their lower ranks.

She said they would provide me with a residence and a small stipend each month, if I could come to take care of my future grandchild. Wow! This meant that trips all over Europe could be possible for me!

CHAPTER 13

Teresa was in military intelligence at the airport connected to the Air Force and "launched" the spy planes during her tour. That was the total knowledge I had about her job. She never shared a sentence of information about her duties. Mike's assignment was in supplies.

My job was to prepare the meals and clean house for the two of them. A German family owned the home and occupied the first floor, Teresa and Mike the second, and Oma (grandmother) lived on the third floor.

Alone, I took my first flight to Germany. From Dallas, I went on to New York, then into Frankfurt. Through glass from a corridor, I saw Teresa and Mike. They looked so good to me. The joy felt was indescribable. After my passport and other things were inspected, my steps quickened toward them. She was big with child. We tearfully embraced, then hurried to get my luggage; but it was lost. We were instructed to have a complimentary lunch and wait for the next plane, which had my luggage on board.

As we enjoyed the lengthy meal, we observed and compared what we saw to the American way. One simple thing was the waiter and the cutlery. The knife was between the tines of the fork. Small things like this attracted my attention. I was in a different "world."

On the ride to my new home, I noticed the branches on the trees hung laden with the winter snow. They looked somewhat like our common cedar trees, yet the branches seemed to hang in the opposite direction than our trees. The snow was also only on one side of the trunk, as if the wind blew in only one direction. The houses appeared to all be of stucco and all had tile roofs. There were neither wood nor brick houses anywhere to be seen.

The front door of each house was individually carved, and the sheer curtains in the windows were all with different tasteful designs.

At night the shutters were closed for warmth and privacy, whereas in America, they were used solely for decoration and secured against the house. Heat was turned off or very low at night.

Many times I compared the atmosphere to America 50 years ago. The shops were closed about noon on Saturdays in all the smaller villages, to be opened again on Mondays. Also, I saw no large trucks driving on the autobahn (highway) on the weekends.

Just as we pulled up to the raised-by-stone yard and wrought iron gate, the car stopped and would not start again. What a relief that it had not stopped on the sharply-curved, in many places, autobahn while I was in the car. Mike and Teresa voiced the same feeling. We were happy that if the car was worn out, it survived long enough to bring me to my new home.

Mike opened the iron gate, and we ascended the first few steps to the short walkway that led to the front door steps. The door was of lovely carved heavy wood that admitted us to a hall that, to the right had doors that opened to the apartment of Herr and Frau Palme. On the left wall were the steps that led up to the second floor, our apartment. We ascended the steps. Just before reaching the top, they rounded sharply to the right, slightly narrow for my comfort. Therefore, the banister at the right top was difficult for me to grip. I would have to take special care on the steps at all times because of my previously injured knees.

Then Mike unlocked the door for us. It was not like American doors; it had handles instead of knobs. (We heard many times that we Americans were called "those people that come from the country with round door handles.") The doors were made of thick glass that admitted only the light.

The home was of sturdy vintage, rebuilt after being bombed during World War II. It was exactly as previously built, but with modern changes. Our entrance hall opened into the one large bathroom. There was a gas heater on the wall that heated the water as it was being used, so that the gas did not go on and off several times a day. This conserved gas. Another glass door led from our entrance hall into the dining room, living room, and into the kitchen. A second glass door from the hall bypassed the dining room to get through the living room into the kitchen.

The stove was half the size of the ones at home. The refrigerator was about the size of those furnished in hotels for beverages and such. For us, a small freezer was added by Herr Palme. The kitchen sink was half size, and the kitchen table was small and oblong. The pantry was another piece of furniture, since Germans were taxed on closets (considered another room in the house). Every inch, it seemed, was used conservatively. French doors led us from the kitchen onto the balcony that ran the length of the rear of the house. At the end of the balcony was another door that opened onto our entrance hall.

We went back inside and revisited the two bedrooms. They each opened onto our private entrance hall. The doors were made of the same thick glass as the others. Of course, wood encircled them. One could make out the shadow of someone on the other side, but not clearly. Our furniture was antique and well-made of heavy wood. My closet was a wardrobe (pronounced "shrunk" in German). In this was hung my clothing. The dresser and "shrunk" drawers held my folded clothes and personals.

My dresser had embroidered, lace-edged doilies, as not seen by me since the 1950s. The bedspread was pure "folk art" design (so beautifully displayed in the area, especially in the Alps). Such was one of the two throw pillows on my single bed. It was heart-shaped and ruffled. Teresa had taken great care to decorate to make me comfortable. My bedroom was in the corner of the house, so my view was over the two intersecting streets and its houses. The baby bed had been placed under one of the two windows, the one closest to my bed.

Drapes of heavy cotton with bold designs covered our bedroom windows and the French doors in the kitchen. All the windows, as well as the French doors opening onto the balcony were of clear glass, so the drapes were drawn at times.

At nighttime, our neighbors had their drapes and the shutters closed for warmth and privacy. If we drove the streets at night, the village seemed vacant. Only the gasthaus (local pub which offered brotchen and bratwurst, beer, coffee and other foods) was lit.

Teresa had stocked the house and made my reception one to always remember. Everything was so foreign to me, and yet it so reminded me of North Nashville in the earlier days of my life. The area had housed many German families there. The streets were so quiet and seemed so safe. This was indeed a wonderful adventure for me, one I had never anticipated in my future.

The next morning after arriving, I was aroused about five a.m. by the loud chipping of metal against concrete. My shutters had not been closed, so I switched on my small lamp and peeped through the drapes. My neighbors across the street were clearing their sidewalks of snow. I learned that it was the German law to remove snow because you were liable for anyone falling. Teresa and Mike tried to familiarize me with the customs and laws throughout my visit.

They took some time off from their work to acclimate me and to get a new car. They chose a car from Sweden. It was indeed comfortable and roomy.

One day Teresa was standing in front of her wardrobe mirror and turned sideways to view her body profile. She sarcastically exclaimed, "Mother, I look like Big Bird on Sesame Street." Of course, my reply was a burst of laughter and an assurance to her that she looked like any other mother-to-be.

They usually left for work very early, long before my waking hour. There was so much to see and absorb in this new environment. I could often see through their windows, the Fraus across the street dusting the insides of their lampshades (a chore we seldom did). One chore that they did that I copied was the weekly (yes, WEEKLY) washing of my windows. They were usually no taller than we could reach and were made of a single piece of glass. Also, they all swung inside, so that we stayed inside the house to wash them. I wanted the Fraus to be proud that an American resided in their neighborhood and that her windows were clean, too.

The windows sparkled with no sign of a smear. They were crystal clear. Teresa had obtained the special cleaning formula from a Frau on base. It was made from everyday household supplies, and it worked.

My first visit to a German superstore with them was interesting. It was snowing a little and was beginning to get dark. Teresa asked me to try a brotchen and bratwurst (their version of a hotdog). It proved to be the most delicious bread and wurst of my life. The bread was as if they had just baked it. Coffee was my choice of beverage, made just the right strength, too. There, with the snow falling I stood, with a cut-high tree stump as my table. What fun!

"Mom, I only wish I had a camera to make your picture roughing it for my sisters to see! I can't believe you standing in the snow eating a hotdog." She laughed heartily as she shook her head in disbelief.

Another treat: they took me downtown to Harry's. He catered to American military. In the store could be found almost any gift item or souvenir of Germany and Europe that could be imagined at a good price.

The thrift stores about town were exciting, especially for children's wear. Most of the items available on the base were of lightweight material, but the German items were well-made and heavy to meet the cold environment. Their kinder (children) were very special to them and were given the best, in most instances. Their baby buggies were well built, durable and comfortable as could be made. Of course, they were expensive and beyond our budget.

The first Christmas in Germany was exciting, though the others of my family were severely missed. We were asked by the Palmes to share the lighting of their tree with them. To my amazement, they had actual candles on the tree tips and lighted them. (I wondered what the fire codes at home would say about us doing that.) It was traditional and exuded the warmth of the season. Considered a tradition to include only their family, we felt honored to be part of it.

Additionally, Teresa said the Palmes had never before rented to enlisted people, only to officers and their families. Upon applying for the apartment, Teresa had to overcome the objection of her rank. Frau Palme relented and accepted them. Then when Teresa told her that she was pregnant and needed her mother there for the baby, more objections were raised, especially about the utilities.

Teresa said that once Frau Palme met me, her disapproval vanished. We became good friends. I went with them to several symphonies (one was a symphony orchestra from Prague), a German play, to watch one of their dance classes (their waltzing was the most enjoyable) and dinners in their home.

For that first Christmas, Teresa and Mike decorated a tree, and we exchanged presents on Christmas Day. Of course, we baked and had the usual feast. It was a strange feeling to be so far away from America on Christmas (or any other day); but it was my intention to enjoy every aspect of life in Europe to which I was privileged. The people and the environment continued to fascinate me.

In March, Jamian, my grandson was born at the hospital in Landstuhl. From our second-floor window the day he was born, I anxiously watched them cross the street and get into the car en route to the hospital. Mike later phoned me that we had a boy in the family.

Nancy, my granddaughter, had been born in Germany to Susan and Gary a few years before. She was a precocious child, the first of my (three-to-be) grandchildren. In Savannah, she was always straying away to the neighbors, looking for a new friend. Nancy loved to bring them home and have me make diamond-shaped sandwiches so they could picnic outside.

She highly amused me by telling me that my legs were "real pretty" (pointing to the colors in my unwanted varicose veins, not understanding why my laughter was so hearty when this compliment was given to me).

When she got up in the mornings, if Robin or her mom and dad were asleep, she would come to my room and wake me to go to the den of the house with her, not wanting to go alone.

"Why are you waking me, sweetheart? Go get your mom or dad to go to the den with you!" My usual sleepy groan.

"They are tarred (tired)," she would reply.

"Call Aunt Robin then!"

Invariably, the answer was, "She's tarred, too."

Because of her blonde naturally curly hair and blue eyes, she could persuade me to do most anything any other doting grandmother would do.

Jamian was kept in the room with his mother instead of the nursery at the hospital. My early arrival at the hospital was welcomed. Naturally, from that day he was with me constantly, except when his mother or dad was home. The weekend or special off days for them usually became a tour into one of the surrounding countries. For me, too.

Paris was interesting, especially Versailles. The day before we went, terrorists had bombed a part of this beautiful place. We did not see the damaged area, but the remainder was utterly fascinating. Much to my embarrassment, a guard loudly admonished me in French for merely touching a drape. At Notre Dame, while photographing the façade it became apparent that no tourists were around me. Looking up to the right, several rows of cars were headed toward me. Then it dawned on me that this was not a plaza but part of the street. What to do since running was out of the question for my knees? Aha!! By putting my right arm extended like an American traffic cop, they stopped for me.

It was always good to cross the border back into Germany on any of my trips... a bit like returning "home." Weekend trips to the countryside of France were enjoyable, and they were many.

Other weekends, we traveled through the German villages. Once we saw a typical quaint village wedding with bride and groom on the wagon, with the wedding guests walking behind. The best of freshly made breads could be found in a town's bakery. They were usually within the town, unmarked, so that only the villagers frequented them. We usually stopped someone and asked for the location. Their parks were outstanding, usually boasting a lake with lovely swans.

During this time, Lisa divorced André. She said he was seeing someone in the trio of singers that opened Charley's shows. This was devastating to us and to his parents. We always stayed friends with them, loving them as we remembered them in their four-month visit with us when we opened the smorgasbord restaurant. Lisa, too, continued to love them with a profound devotion.

Lisa moved from Dallas to Oklahoma to be near Susan. There, she met and married Randy. He was in the Army and Lisa was soon to move to Germany with him. They were to live in the Bavarian area (Ulm, Germany).

During Gary's second Army tour in Germany, Nancy played with the German children so much, she could speak the language fluently. As my abbreviated study of the language grew, I would speak my few words to Jamian to make him familiar with them, too. He was so young, he would just questionably look at me. Even so, I practiced my limited vocabulary on him anyway. We often watched the children from the second-floor window as they went to school, and I would speak to him only in German.

Our many late afternoon jaunts, with me pushing him in his stroller, took us over several street blocks. This was after his parents had come home for the day or on some weekends. Because we were usually dressed in their clothes by choice of quality (via the thrift store), passersby would greet us in German. My blundering response would immediately let them know we were American. They always smiled with understanding at my feeble attempts to speak their language.

Lisa soon announced that she was pregnant. The army sent her to the best German doctors, because they learned that something was wrong with the fetus. At delivery, I was at the hospital in the Bavarian area. The baby, Clair, was taken to the German hospital, and there were some doubts about her survival. Though with some birth defects, she blossomed into a lovely little girl. She was intelligent, and her physical problems were not apparent at all. This was an answer to prayers, many prayers.

Now, I had three grandchildren. All were born in Germany into three military families.

Again, my health began to bother me. My blood pressure was rising. Another carotid artery operation was mentioned by my doctors at Landstuhl. Because my rest was vital, the care of Jamian had to be shared with someone. A phone call to Robin was the answer. She had entered college in Savannah, but said she would drop out and join us. I told her the doctor feared another artery blockage, again on the left side. The thought frightened me to have the surgery done in a foreign country, away from my Nashville families.

Robin arrived in Germany within days. In the meantime, after much pleading with my doctor to allow me to try to lower my blood pressure with better diet and habits, he granted me a delay with close follow-ups. I experienced my first Doppler examination in his office. He would merely run the "microphone" over my neck on the left side. There was no pain, but a lot of loud gushing of blood could be heard. The test reassured him the surgery could be delayed. Was it coincidence that he was graduated at Meharry in Nashville? Dr. Walker released a grateful patient, but not until after many referrals to be sure his prognosis was acceptable.

Jamian took to Robin, and Robin took to Europe. All around, it was love at first sight. She rented a kitchenette/bedroom/living room, bath and tiny balcony near us. It was small, but comfortable. With her winning personality, she became fast friends with Uli, the son of a doctor's widow. He attended the University nearby, but later would graduate and go to Berlin to work with Americans on lasers.

She borrowed Uli's car to drive Jamian and me all over the countryside. The car was red and very small. It was an English mini. When we would come out of the apartment for an outing and Jamian was in Robin's arms, he would point to the mini, urging her with grunts and struggles toward it instead of the larger car owned by his parents.

It was good to have her there for many reasons. A special one was after a fall at the laundromat when my knee gave out (or my foot slipped on something). Even a bed sheet placed on my leg hurt, as light as it was. She was there every day for us, cleaning and cooking, taking up my duties. Also, she was a perfect companion for weekend tours by bus.

Many times we visited Lisa in Ulm. This always provided a happy time, to visit my youngest child and watch

Clair grow, seemingly healthy in every noticeable way. She lived among several tall apartment buildings, each apartment usually owned by its occupant. In her particular building resided only servicemen and their families. The soldiers were connected with a missile site somewhere in Bavaria.

On a visit to Lisa, I was washing dishes at the kitchen sink. It overlooked an extended narrow public balcony that ran alongside the kitchen windows and led to other apartments. Her apartment was on the first floor. The tops of the huge metal trash bins were visible. A boy about ten years old opened the glass door from the entrance hall, held the door for a moment and surveyed the trash bins. This was unusual. Then he disappeared, apparently taking the elevator to a top floor.

Shortly, I caught a side glimpse of something falling. On closer inspection, the boy was apparently dropping garbage bags from his balcony to keep from making several trips to the bins.

I chuckled. This was an example of American ingenuity, but certainly not the type his mother had envisioned when she assigned him the chore.

When Lisa returned I related the incident to her. She didn't think it very amusing, so she asked me to describe the boy and forthwith visited his mother that evening. Needless to say, much of the trash from outside was eliminated from that time on. It embarrassed Lisa to learn that the Germans would say, "If you want to find out which is the American Building, just follow the litter!"

On my later return to America, my awareness of litter on the streets or anywhere was intent. This was echoed by my nephew, Gene, and his wife, Chris, who had also lived in Germany for many years prior to my going. There seemed to be no litter anywhere, they also said.

Our apartment on many Sundays was home away from home for some of the fellow soldiers, especially Teresa's. For them, it was usually a full meal served buffet style; they were grateful for these "homey" meals. Soon, she requested cookies or cakes to take to them each week at work as an additional treat. One especially fond memory was maneuver time. She said my sweets were divided up, with the ground crews carrying them by truck, and the pilots carrying them under their seats in the planes until they reached their destinations. She chuckled when she told me that one pilot took his box of goodies with him to the restroom before departing, so that he could keep his eye on them at all times. This incident really did "touch" me, especially as a mother.

Teresa planted flowers in the window boxes in the spring. She hung them over the rails of the back balcony. It was most enjoyable to water them, pinch them back and enjoy the blooms. Especially delightful were the cascading red geraniums, planted profusely in each box. During my adult life, there seemed to be no time for anything but working and running the house. My duties had always been multiple, with no time for raising flowers. This privilege was not afforded me before Germany. It was as though that here was presented an opportunity to indulge a hobby or pursue an art. Ah, here was another revelation of growing older: to admire the people who so effortlessly grew flowers and visited each other day after day and made time for this somehow...

Teresa announced that she was leaving the Army, a little sooner than Mike and would return to the states with Jamian. Neither Robin nor I was ready to return; we wanted to see more of the countries. When Teresa departed, we took a house in a small nearby village with a very personable woman named Cathy Smith. She was with the Air Force. We equally shared the rent and other expenses, with me again doing most of the preparation of meals.

Robin met and dated several eligible young men, but did not seem as interested in any as much as the Lt. Colonel Chris Christianson that she brought home one evening to meet Cathy and me. She was also charmed by a young Captain who flew a "tank killer." Sid's home in America was Boston. They vied for Robin's attention. Soon, Sid was transferred to England, but kept in close touch with her. He was constantly entreating her to bring me, saying that he wanted the two of us to be his guests there. He tried many proposals, in order to be near her. She declined, however, the phone calls and communications kept coming to Robin.

One day there was a knock at her door. Robin answered to two officers bearing bad news from England. They told her Sid was departing a petrol station in his sports car and was hit by a passing car. He was killed instantly. Then they presented a box with an engagement ring that Sid had purchased in Holland for Robin. He had told them that he was going to ask for her hand in marriage on his next visit to her. She was pained by the loss of Sid and surprised that he was going to ask her to marry him. After caressing the ring for a moment, she gave it back to them, "Please give it to his mother; it would mean so much to her." Tearfully, she mumbled her appreciation and closed the door.

Chris purchased the well-kept car from Teresa and Mike and sold his big car, having been too huge for the narrow quaint streets. Mike moved back to barracks when Teresa left, and no longer needed the car.

When Robin and Chris asked me along for volks-marching, this was a treat. Knowing that my knees could not tolerate the exercise, they usually accompanied friends off on the march while I stayed behind, observed the people and ate. The marches (hikes) usually lasted about three hours, sometimes more.

Many times, they would go with Jim and Suzette, and come home later to my prepared meal for them all. (Jim and Suzette were both Colonels in the Army; he was in hospital administration and she was a nurse.) After the meal we sat in the backyard. It was always most entertaining to hear Chris and Jim swap stories, usually leaving me in a fit of laughter. They were both astute in delivering the punch lines with a very wry humor. Suzette spoke several languages, English with a heavy accent, and did not always understand the American clowning. Or maybe she chose to ignore it? Anyway, she smiled with her toleration.

For the march, they each earned a medal. The medal was designed/ engraved for the particular village at the end of the march. Each was individual and desired. Many Sunday afternoons found me waiting in the backyard for their return and the always pleasant visits.

Another special trip was to Innsbruck, Austria. Robin and I were guests of Chris, and we stayed at a hotel with the other officers and wives. At one formal dinner, we were the only two women at our table. It was enchanting to have all the officers stand each time I arose from our table and each time I returned. I was always graciously seated. To be surrounded by so many charming men in uniform, hanging on to every word we said, was a never-to-be-forgotten evening. The entertainment was folk dancing and music, all Austrian.

We also attended other parties. At one, the General of the European command was introduced to me and we chatted. Later, at a dinner party at another hotel, he was leaving a meeting he led with other officers and noticed me at the nearby table. We smiled, and I slightly lifted my hand to wave. On stage an Austrian pianist had been entertaining us in the very crowded room as we dined. As he walked, surrounded by officers, he failed to notice the end of the pianist's stage and caught his foot there. He stumbled forward and was immediately kept from a tumble by some quick-thinking assistants. Gasps could be heard. Embarrassed that I had caused this stir, I quickly glanced behind me as if looking to see to whom he was waving. All at my table knew, but no one said anything. On a later day, Chris ran into him, and he asked about me. He jokingly added, "She is the first woman I almost broke my neck over."

CHAPTER 14

One day a call from Teresa came to me. She wanted me to return to the states to help with Jamian. He seemed to be unhappy with various childcare placements, always crying when she left him to go to school or work each day. They were both unhappy and confused.

About the same time, my dear friend, Margit, came for a visit to us from the states. She asked me to go to Vienna, Austria for a visit with acquaintances. They were connected with her church and served as missionaries and provided shelter for those escaping the Iron Curtain. They were also involved in the printing and distribution of Bibles into Soviet-occupied countries. This sounded exciting to me. To be able to visit Vienna had always been a dream of mine.

Margit visited us in Bahn for a few days, then I bade Robin and Lisa farewell for a time. It was impossible to determine when I would see them again, as I would be returning to the states when my visit to Vienna was over.

Trains carried Margit and me into Vienna. We arrived at a stately-looking old home that was comprised of large apartments. It was situated right on the street, with Anna Marie and "Fahtie" (pronounced fah-tea) occupying the huge corner unit. We were welcomed with a typical European meal and Margit sharing the latest news from America, in the German language, of course. Occasionally, my limited grasp of German allowed me more than just a smile in return to them. Olga, Margit's sister, joined us from Bratislava, a city about 40 miles from Vienna. It was in Soviet-held Czechoslovakia.

Olga was always interesting to me from the first time meeting her in America during a visit to Margit. Her husband was an architect, and her only child, Milan, was studying to be a doctor. Olga carried herself as a true ballerina, with back erect and chin lifted, always slender and chic. She danced at the opera house each evening, after multiple hours of daily practice. She fascinated me. Milan was energetic, outgoing and handsome, towering in height over his mother and father. From childhood, he delighted in tearing things apart and reassembling them. He was full of mischief, none knowing what to expect from him. Soon, I should be meeting him and his father again.

Within a couple of days, Margit, Anna Marie, and I went to the Czech embassy to get our visas to enter Czechoslovakia. Margit was turned down because she was a former Czech citizen.

Anna Marie warned me not to talk to anyone there except to answer questions for my visa. My purse was stripped of anything relating to the military before we left her apartment. (At that time, three of my daughters were married to military men, and the fourth was engaged to one. This information made Anna Marie very nervous.) Inside the embassy, during my wait to be called to the window to be questioned, a woman in her late 20s with a child sat opposite me and began to chat.

Eventually, her questions were directed toward my being an American and why was I going to Czechoslovakia? Were relatives there? (From the corner of my eye, I noted that Anna Marie was exiting.)

The questions did not seem to be of a casual, interested nature, or "small talk." Sensing this, my answers were quick, filled with a lot of gibberish about being overwhelmed to get the privilege of seeing Czechoslovakia, known to be the jewel of Europe at one time. This was true; I was sincerely appreciative for the privilege.

Though true, every effort had to be made to avoid revealing that this was now my third year in Europe and with connections to the military with missiles pointed to their country, no less. My desired impression was to be of an older lady who had just come to Europe for a few days. Apparently it worked; I must have seemed harmless. Eventually, she disappeared. My visa came through without any problems.

Back at Anna Marie's home, it was decided that I would personally take Margit's passport to Prague. They had told her at the embassy it would be two weeks before clearance from Prague could be accomplished; however, Margit wanted us to be on the way home by then.

That night, we conveyed to Andrés parents in Prague that Margit was having a visa problem and would they meet Olga and me at the train station early the next morning? It was agreed that family members would be there, and that when we left the police station, we must visit them.

We promised to do that on a later trip with Margit.

We were met at the train on arrival in Prague by two of Andrés lovely cousins. My language was in English, but they spoke Czech through Olga to me. When the early morning darkness faded, we departed the station and went to the police station. There, questions were asked of me and about Margit. Soon, they gave me several papers to which a photo of me was attached to each. We returned to Vienna with Margit's visa approval.

Some few days were spent going in and out of Bratislava, since Margit now had her visa. On one trip, my luggage was a maroon color, my men's leather jacket matched it, my gold watch was a man's, my men's necklace was gold, and my money was of an unknown amount by me (as it was all for Olga). She shook from fright on the train and had to take some tranquilizers. No problem for me, since this was a new adventure, believing that God would see me through this. I felt it was my small part to contribute to Milan's medical degree. Looking back, I suppose my ignorance of the magnitude of my boldness kept me from being afraid.

We visited with Olga's family in Bratislava. Olga's husband was slightly taller than she, spoke in soft tones and was always kind. He smiled often; this made him an excellent husband for the energetic Olga.

They spoke in the Slovak language, so I had many questions as to what they were talking about. Much to Milan's mother's chagrin, he was constantly making wisecracks about the government. This was the norm for America, but certainly not over there. The adults were aware of the penalties that could ensue. If he was in the kitchen at their apartment, the curtains were closed and the radio was turned on apparently for privacy. My "comments" were usually only chuckles when the jokes were interpreted. Milan was too young to realize the possible consequences, or he was very brave.

My visit to Mother and Father Cejka's was unforgettably pleasant. Lovely framed paintings adorned the house, especially the living room. The furniture was beautiful, reminding me of the prosperity they must have once enjoyed. Father said the Nazi invasion had interrupted a showing of his works that were intended for Paris. He implied that he was not allowed to remove from the country any of his paintings done by him or others from that time on. At first it was the Nazi government, now the Communist.

Margit and I stayed in the apartment downstairs that Lisa and André occupied when they first married. It was lovely, as Lisa had described. Mother gave me a box of pictures that André had made of our restaurant, but she kept the videos that he had made in the past. Father took me for a walk across the Charles River... a walk I shall never forget. It was beautiful...

On a subsequent trip to Prague, while they stayed at their villa, Margit and I were treated to the penthouse of one of the country music entertainers and his lovely wife (who looked like one of our movie stars and could have easily passed for her sister). They were also movie stars behind the Iron Curtain. One of their hits was the Jack London movie, "Call of the Wild."

During that visit, we went to a small town where our friends (a different band) gave an annual benefit performance. We passed one of the most notorious prison camps of Hitler's reign in Europe. It reminded me of the gloomy day I visited Dachau several months before. I kept my sunglasses on so that no one would notice my tears. On our way back to Prague, the car's occupants became sober. The night was black, heavy with the midnight hour. The mood was different than that of the exuberance displayed by the appreciative musical audience of a few hours before. Margit and I were seated for the performance in a private balcony, because we were "special" guests. Whispers and glances greeted us, since the village wondered why Americans had decided to also visit them. My curiosity was just as keen, since this was my first visit to a small Czech village.

The bands entertained us one night and treated us to a delicious lunch another day. The entire visit was one to remember.

As we walked with the movie star through Prague, cameras clicked. Doting fans rarely saw him in public. We passed a gift shop and he insisted upon my selection of a gift; I chose some small hand-carved cups.

At the luncheon, and also at the penthouse, some of the band members spoke of defecting. My comments were rare, for fear of being overheard. Later, the actor did escape to America by one route, and the wife and son by another. Even though they entertained in Russia, Poland, Hungary, among all the Communist countries, the three were never permitted to leave the country together. I was told the son had to stay behind to ensure their return.

Shopping was interesting. The items for sale were few, displayed as if the store was upper end and each item priceless. There was very little of anything to buy. The one store that seemed to be well-stocked was the one that accepted only money from the free world. It appeared the local people could not afford to go into it.

I was often approached on the street to buy their money at a far better rate than the legitimate banks offered, especially after they heard me speak and determined that I was an American. They were politely ignored, for obvious reasons.

At a depot on one of our ventures, our luggage was put aboard a small motorized open cart to be driven to the train at the opposite end of the station, a long walk. In broken English, the young driver spoke, patted the seat next to him and offered me a ride, "You, American. I want to live in America. I am happy to see you." I smiled and climbed aboard. He drove me through the crowds (reminding me of the parting of the Red Sea, as they stepped aside to let us through). The others in my group had to walk behind us. When they did finally overtake us, Olga was nervous, afraid his comments had been overheard by the wrong people.

We took an exciting trip into Budapest, Hungary. After spending the night, we toured the city. One church that we visited was the most outstanding seen by me in Europe. The architecture embraced many of the cultures in Hungary's history.

The seriousness of the people and the fact they seldom smiled, moved me. (This reminded me of a photo my son-in-law, Gary, had sent me before coming to Germany.

It showed the towers that housed the soldiers guarding the Czech borders. "The world's biggest prison," he had noted on the backside of the picture.)

On one return trip to Vienna alone, my greeter at the train was to be someone new. Margit had given me a vague description of him. Noted on this trip, when we arrived at the border where the Czech armed guards got off, were the multiple (more than usual) Austrian guards boarding. On arrival at the station (by the privileged few, allowed to leave), we were met by dozens of heavily armed guards.

A smiling man approached me when I disembarked, "Are you Clara?" To my relief, he fitted the description of my rendezvous. After appropriate introductions, I noted we were being surrounded by armed guards. Alongside us and around us, the guards kept up as we walked.

"Gwin, why the escorts?"

"Last Saturday's train was met by terrorists, and everyone aboard was killed. I heard they were killing all Jews and refugees aboard. So, they're not taking any chances this week," he solemnly answered me.

Margit was in the Alps and was not expected for a couple of days.

During this visit to Vienna, I visited the palace, quipping on the way in, "Wonder how many years of my life it would take to clean this house from one end to the other?"

It was lovely, beautiful beyond description.

Later, a friend in the states said that one of my classmates had married there in Vienna. Napoleon's carriage and the Viennese symphony orchestra were used for the occasion. His bride was said to be one of the world's richest women.

Mrs. Gwin gave me a personal tour through the museum. Once following several groups of individual tours, one of the last members of the group turned to me and said, "You are so fortunate to have your own personal guide. I've been listening to her instead of our guide. She seems more informed." I smiled and nodded my head in agreement.

Upon entering that morning, I chose to leave my raincoat on. It was explained that if you had a coat on upon arrival, you were required to keep it on. Carrying it was not permitted. On going alone into a small room of glass-enclosed treasures and elegant wall hangings, I noted a young couple was there also. Suddenly the alarm in the room sounded. The couple exited quickly. Immediately, a security guard rushed in, sternly noticed my presence, and closely followed me until I left the museum that day. It was amusing to me, since nothing had been touched and my coat was still buttoned. Being privileged to see these huge and rare treasures would linger always in my mind, as well as the suspicion that I was perhaps an art thief.

The grandeur of the palace reminded me of my visit to Paris several months before. The awe shall always remain at seeing The Hall of Mirrors and the handiwork of Marie Antoinette's many brothers and sisters, who were each taught a trade in the event they needed it in the future. Her mother was a wise ruler. No wonder, she reigned so many years.

When Margit returned from the Alps, my trips into Czechoslovakia were completed, so we decided to return to America.

Our friends were still printing Bibles in Vienna as we departed, and smuggling them into the communist countries, risking life and limb. "Fahtie" (forced to serve in the German army under Hitler) had been in an automobile accident in Russia on one such "run." His car was hit by a drunken Russian officer. Injuries were chiefly confined to his ribs area. He was put into a cast there. On returning home, the doctors in Vienna were horrified to find the wet plaster cast had been put directly onto his skin. When they removed it to correct the treatment already given, they pulled the skin away with the plaster. Fortunately, he survived, but was told if he ever returned over the border and they did not catch him, they would enter Vienna, kidnap him, and he would never again be seen. After that, he remained in Vienna directing the printing but did not go back in for any deliveries. He never stopped helping to house and find a home for those who fled Communism, affirming that this was his Christian mission.

On my flight home, I related to Margit an amusing incident concerning my luggage. Mike and Teresa were on military leave, and we decided to go home to America for a visit. My major piece of luggage would not fit into the trunk of the car, so it was decided that it would be strapped on top. "Remember, there is no speed limit on the autobahn!" I added. " As usual, cars were zipping by us at breakneck speed, unbelievable, terrifying if you really thought about it ."

Previously, I related how Robin enjoyed chauffeuring Jamian and me around the countryside. Sometimes we would venture onto the autobahn, but that came to a screeching halt. The little red English mini (with exceptionally small tires, I thought) didn't have much engine pickup. When we occasionally dared to enter the autobahn, got exceptionally brave, and decided to pull around a slow car in front of us, THAT was a joke! (We only pulled around when we were on level road.) Invariably... anytime we got about halfway around, a car from out of nowhere would pull up behind us with flashing lights, viciously impatient, demanding that they pass us. Usually, we dropped back to where we were. (Remember, too, that we had German license plates on that mini!) After half a dozen or more attempts, we'd give up and go back to the little roads to reach our destination. We gave up traveling on the autobahn.

"Oh, Margit, the funny part about my luggage on my visit home—we were cruising right along when Mike suddenly yelled, 'Granny's luggage just flew off.' Sure enough, it was three lanes over. What to do?

"Mike came to a halt in the emergency stop area. After a brief exchange with Teresa, he jumped out of the car. He surveyed the menacing problem and started across the autobahn to retrieve my suitcase. I expected it to be crushed over and over by ongoing traffic. Somehow, the cars were getting over it or around it—skilled driving, I guess. Once Mike started, I couldn't look any more. I closed my eyes and softly, intently prayed for his safety, and did not open them again until I heard his voice at the car. My prayers were answered: he was safe and unharmed—and so was my suitcase. He secured it on top of the car once more, and off we went to board our plane for the United States.

"That piece made it through customs in Boston, our flight to Nashville and transfer of planes for me to go to Oklahoma to visit with Susan for a few days. She met me at the airport, drove me to her home and, as she took the luggage from her car's trunk, it fell apart. We laughed in disbelief that it had held together... simply amazing. Needless to say, she gave me one of her lovely pieces to replace it. I liked my new piece much better than the old luggage."

On my arrival back in America, my residence was with Teresa and Jamian. Mike was discharged from the Army a few months later and joined us. My primary duties were to watch after Jamian until he could eventually adjust to being away from me.

Soon after Mike's return, he and Teresa divorced.

Teresa, Jamian, and I shared an apartment on the west side of town. It was located near the University. She wanted to return to college and change her area of study in pursuit of a livable career.

After graduation, she took a brief holiday to see her sister, Susan. The military had again transferred Gary back to Oklahoma. On her return, she transferred planes for Nashville in Dallas. There, Teresa encountered her Major from the intelligence unit in which she served during her Army stint.

On her arrival back in Nashville, she excitedly told me of their meeting, "Mother, he asked me what I was doing. I told him I had just graduated.

"My answer was negative to having a job, so he suggested a job is available to me if I will move to Dallas. Since my security clearance is in order, it will be no problem. My duties will be associated with classified security projects."

She grinned broadly when she said, "He told me to tell you not to call him 'Major Moore.' He said to be sure to tell you that before discharge his rank was Colonel!" (To me, he affectionately would always be "Major Moore," one of the Army's finest.)

During the time Teresa was in college, Robin married the Lt. Col. Chris, she met in Germany. His home was Minneapolis.

Chris retired to accept a job under his previous Colonel and dear friend, Jim, in management in Riyadh, Saudi Arabia's royal guard hospital. Robin worked there in the computer area. It was difficult to be confined to the compound, but she adjusted well to the customs.

Robin delighted in telling about the honor system of getting your own gas and leaving the money, about the fancy cars abandoned by the road, and having to be escorted everywhere she went. She told me about a goat's eyes presented in Jim's honor and how Jim, at his request, had them passed on to her. This was an important dinner, so she graciously accepted and ate them.

"Mother, apparently my stomach is stronger than his, and he knew my curiosity was overwhelming anyway." She said that prior to dinner time, there was this noisy banging in the preparation area, where obviously this goat was being prepared for the feast.

The customs fascinated her, but she missed her freedom; this was apparent. Her love for all peoples showed true in the descriptions of her environment.

That first autumn, one of my letters contained two of the prettiest leaves that had fallen from our trees. Robin phoned from Saudi, gushing with thanks for them. She had put them in her office, and word spread through the hospital that real U.S. tree leaves were there. They were left attached to her bulletin board for all to see, and there were many with whom she shared that taste of home.

CHAPTER 15

The thought occurred to me that I would like to see American balconies, especially the barren looking apartment rails, laden with flowers growing from overhanging planters as seen in Europe, especially Germany. Just as with my idea for the restaurant, plans had to be made to produce the desired result. For weeks, each step toward the project was developed and evaluated by me. In a lengthy letter, single-spaced typing of several pages, the idea was presented to Robin and Chris asking for money to get the plans drawn and hire a patent attorney. My planters were to be of excellent quality and features not seen on the market.

My product would have a not-to-be forgotten name, a name, hopefully, that customers and potential customers could easily identify. (I remember this came up when Margit and I discussed what her restaurant should be called. She wanted to call it the Bountiful Bord. I contended that it should bear the name of the area. Then, when people heard about its good food, they would know where it was located. Since it was the Hermitage area of Nashville, I suggested simply Hermitage House Smorgasbord. She liked the name. By the same token, upon choosing a name for my restaurant, I used the same reasoning: Hendersonville House Smorgasbord.) The catchy name for my flower planter would be the Blumen Box. This word was German for flowers. If someone said, "Bloomin' idiot," or "The flowers are bloomin'," they would, hopefully, think of my product. Pronunciation of the word Blumen is blooming, without the "g."

Robin and Chris could see the possibilities in my idea and sent me a check to get started.

As the project progressed, it became apparent to me that this "item" that appeared to be so simple was, instead, an enormous undertaking. There were the problems of manufacturing, a mold to be made, shipping/display boxes, and all associated packaging, art and photo work, brochure, brackets, measurements so that everything fit, weights, colors, nuts (bolts, screws), salesmen, volume buyers, a fair price for Mom-and-Pop shops to make them competitive with the volume buyers, etc. etc. etc. etc. The deeper the involvement, the more the challenge.

Too, I wanted the best planter product on the market. It was to be durable, have good tubular drainage, and have a grained exterior that wouldn't fade in the sun. The brackets had to be color matched and expandable.

When Teresa could spare time from school studies and sharing responsibility of Jamian, we worked on various phases of the project. We kept and shared the same apartment, so one side of the dining room was turned into an office.

After Teresa left for her job in Dallas, Robin and Chris came home to stay. Their contract was up in Saudi Arabia. They took an apartment near me, and Robin began to share my enthusiasm for the Blumen Box. She drove me everywhere, since a car could not be afforded by me. Soon, they bought a house and invited me to move in with them.

The production of five colors had to be reduced to two, because it meant saving a few dollars on an order that could be passed on to the wholesale buyer. At every opportunity, we sought to make a quality product at the best price, which meant we were constantly examining the costs. Each part of the product came from a different source and had to be assembled at the plant that produced the planter.

Condition of the finished product would sometimes cause us to move to another manufacturer, or the discovery of better workmanship at a lesser price. The problems were daily challenges, constantly changing. Too, we spent several weeks traveling thousands of miles to personally talk to store buyers.

The initial vision of seeing beautiful flowers cascading from windows and balconies all over the country never left me. I could visualize easy gardening, not having to stoop over, boxes at waist level... even the handicapped could tend them from a wheelchair. I could see the joy this simple "gardening" could bring to so many people who could not dig in an outside garden for whatever their reason. As with the restaurant, I sought and got investment by means of selling stock. I had to start out small until the business proved itself and I could go "public."

Association with Ralph, employed by one of our local TV stations, took us to his home in Pennsylvania. With him, Robin and I visited with two professional baseball players, were guests along with the other families in the lounge outside their locker room, as well as the ball games. This was a treat we were to relish all our lives. I was presented a baseball signed by each player on one of the teams. We saw the Cincinnati Reds ballgame, and traveled to St. Louis for the second pro game. Ralph's television career moved him to Pennsylvania permanently, but he never lost his positive vision for Blumen. He, too, was consumed by the possibilities of the product.

Unfortunately, my health began to wane again. Already, there had been several surgeries, and there were more in the picture ahead. It was too premature for anyone to seriously consider buying Blumen, so Blumen folded. Again, my heart was broken. My thoughts of seeing the barren balconies bloom in the spring were gone. The challenges had to be replaced with calm thoughts of personal survival. My future existence depended upon it.

My social life seemed to center around trips to the doctors, hospital and physical therapy. Robin was very patient, and Chris would constantly tease me about bricking me up in my bedroom. Church would be by television. Grocery shopping to compare prices and present clipped coupons also were "the high" on my social calendar, when my health allowed it.

Invitations out were ignored, because I didn't want to burden anyone with the inconvenience of assisting me or having to drive me. I had not operated a vehicle in years. Robin and Chris took care of my needs cheerfully.

Lisa frequently took me for weekends to her home. Visits to Teresa in Dallas and Susan in Oklahoma were rare, but we phoned often.

When old friends, seldom seen, would call on me or encounter me at the store or doctor's office, the subject usually went to why remarriage had not been sought in my life during these many years of being a widow. Robin would usually respond with, "She has always looked the other way," but my answer would be that rearing four daughters alone had taken my time, and what man in his right mind would want a woman with four children?

Pretending dismay at my indifference, Robin would inject that I expected Prince Charming to knock on my front door any day and declare with open arms, "Here I am, the prize for whom you have been waiting all these years." Laughter always followed that remark from all within earshot.

Over the years, I never dated. Privately, I carried the thought that I never wanted to be "possessed, owned, ruled over, or manipulated" again. I had earned my freedom, and wanted to keep it. Furthermore, I was convinced and kept saying to myself and others, "Most of the good men are already taken, and I don't want to go out there and face the stiff competition for those good men that are not already taken." I was at peace with myself, because I knew, after much self-examination, that I had done everything possible to make my marriage work, and resolved to spend the rest of my life alone. But that resolve was to change.

CHAPTER 16

In the early months of 2001, my dear classmate, Mattie Lou, had phoned, as in each previous year, to urge me to attend the annual June high school reunion. The graduating classes represented were from 1941 through 1966. Seeing my old friends would be wonderful, we both agreed. Robin was going to Florida with Lisa at that time, and lamented the fact that she could not be there to assure my attendance.

"Mother, you must go! Remember Robert said that the good time had by your 1946 class at our restaurant started this idea of reunion of all the classes? So, what is your excuse? Chris will drop you off at the hotel that night, and Mattie Lou will see that you get home in her car."

"Robin, I simply don't want to go on my walker, and I certainly don't dare to go without it," I retorted. She ignored my reply.

Mattie Lou soon followed her first call with more urging, but my rebuttal was that my pride kept me from going because the use of a walker was necessary for me now. She replied that it should not be a problem. After all, Marvin Pugh would be there, and he had both of his legs off. To my horror, she told me he had lost them in the Korean War.

After the shock of that realization, my first thought was why should she be so interested in my presence there? After all, his older brother had dated her older sister, and Marvin had dated Mattie Lou a few times when we were in school together. She was a widow now and, I believe, she said that Marvin was a widower. She should try to renew their old friendship, I thought.

I could visualize that Marvin would be in a wheelchair. His loss was due to service to our country, and it seemed that my complaint paled in comparison to his. (So, there was no excuse for me not to go to the reunion.)

That lovely Saturday night in June, Chris dropped me off at the crowded hotel. He escorted me to the door, making sure of my safe entrance. Immediately, dear Mattie Lou saw and approached me, beaming at my arrival (Ha!... actually "showing up"). She must've been very pleased with herself that she "got me out of the house."

The place was so filled, and greetings were so numerous, the fact that someone had taken my walker and brought me a wheelchair to better maneuver me through the crowd didn't register with me. Someone was pushing, but there was no time to determine who it was. Not until my wheelchair was pushed under the table was there time to acknowledge the individual's kindness. It was Marvin Pugh. How could this be that he was pushing me? He sat down between Mattie Lou and me at a roundtable that seated six others.

After dinner, all Korean veterans were each called to the front and a brief summary of their individual sacrifices was given by the Master of Ceremonies. Marvin's service record was unusually outstanding. When he returned to the table, I asked for his e-mail address so that my daughter, Robin, could get some first-hand information that she could possibly use in a fiction story she was writing. He quickly wrote it on the back of my program sheet. We got busy talking to the individuals and groups on opposite sides. Because he was busy talking to Mattie Lou, his back was toward me.

They seemed to be deep in conversation most of the evening. Once, I thought I would help Cupid, and leaned around so that he could hear me and quipped, "Mattie Lou talks about you all the time." (Truly, she did speak of him over the years when I visited her. Max would often tease that he and her sister's husband got 'mighty tired' of hearing about those wonderful Pugh boys. I don't remember ever commenting, just laughing at his remarks about them.)

Marvin did not acknowledge my remark. Soon the band began to play and couples began to dance. I got caught up in the music, thoroughly enjoying it all.

Later, noting that Marvin was gone, I asked, "Where did Marvin go?" Mattie Lou replied that he had gone home. My conclusion was that he had a very busy social life, since he was "available." He had no noticeable limp that I could see. I concluded to myself: guess he had a "pressing date," and left early for that—probably has a date every night.

When Robin returned on Sunday evening from Florida, she was full of questions about the reunion.

While chatting away about the marvelous homecoming with old friends (coined by me as being "some of the best people created by God."), I gave her the program with Marvin's e-mail address and suggested that she at sometime contact him for some book ideas. She already knew about him through my mentioning of not being embarrassed to go to the reunion on a walker, since he would probably be there in a wheelchair. I described him and added he was still shy, but the past 55 years had changed him into a dignified man with no obvious disability. I further commented that I learned his legs were off just below the kneecaps.

"Can you imagine the courage, to walk about as if on stilts all the time? He even pushed my wheelchair into the dining room. Not until the chair was pushed under the table, did I get a glimpse of who was behind me. He is so quiet—just as when he was in school.

"We all had a wonderful time. The memory of this night will stay with me... so dear to me to see their faces again and recall those not here anymore... thank you for making me go."

Robin had told Chris to see that I went, even if I had to go in pajamas. The night out with such old friends would be unforgettable. (None of us realized how true that statement would ring.).

For the next two weeks, Robin spent a great deal of time at the computer, usually in the mornings. Since she was working on her book, this was not uncommon. She told me that she had been e-mailing and asking questions of Marvin about the wars (he was also in World War II). Because of her respect for him, she said she always addressed him as "Sir," and that he was constantly admonishing her that his name was "Marvin" and not "Sir." They apparently had become well acquainted on the computer.

"Robin, it's good that you contacted him. I have wanted to send him an e-mail to thank him for what he did for this country. Apologetically, I want to explain that I lost touch with our classmates over the years and did not know of his wounds. The other night, Pat, the MC, saved Marvin's accolades until last, because his combat was so unusual." She thought that it was a splendid idea to write him.

A couple of days passed before approaching Robin, "Would you tell me how to turn on the computer, and would you show me how to use it, please? I have written only one e-mail before, and that was a letter to Teresa in Dallas. So, please oversimplify the instructions and show me how to write Marvin! Stand by to see if it is okay. OK?"

In the letter were my thanks and an apology for being so negligent about not acknowledging his heroism, and that I was so proud that he was a classmate. I added that no reply was expected nor anticipated because he surely must have a busy life.

Robin called out to me the next day from the computer room, "Mother, your classmate asked for your phone number. He has been asking so many questions about you, the war information is shrinking," she added with a giggle. "I told him you lived with me and our numbers were the same. He was so gallant. He then asked me if he could call upon you. Of course, I told him he could. He will be calling you today."

Sure enough, he phoned me and asked if and when he could come over to visit. We set a time for the next afternoon.

Chris and Robin sat with us about the first 15 minutes to get acquainted, then they excused themselves to busy in another part of the house.

We asked about what the other had been doing the past 55 years. He told me that he had married his high school love, Helen. The marriage of 52 years had ended with her death from Alzheimer's disease. He also revealed that he kept her home with him during the last seven years. I wanted to weep for both of them. A mental picture came to me as I remembered her—a beautiful, vivacious girl of 17, passing her many times in the school hallway.

Marvin was no more than three inches taller than I. His once coal-black thick hair and eyebrows were now gray and thin. His glasses were somewhat darkened as they adjusted to the sunlight indirectly coming through the glass French doors. His piercing eyes were somewhat sad, but bright. They seldom strayed; they were deep dark brown. I liked them. They were honest eyes, not darting, but steady—"windows of the soul"...—he was slight of build, and certainly without the extra pounds I needed to shed. He startled me by often crossing his legs. How could he do this? I noticed there was an indenture at both knees, that suggested a bandage or a bulk of some kind, and assumed this was where the prostheses were connected to the upper thighs.

He smiled and laughed often, usually with a slight curve of one corner of his lips. This man was utterly charming. His skin was wrinkled with a dark tan, suggesting that he spent a great deal of time in the sun. Not true, I was later to learn. He just simply tanned easily from his gardening and frequent games of golf (compliments of his inheritance from an American Indian grandmother and a Spanish grandfather on the maternal side of the family).

I had chosen the couch opposite him, so that I could face him when I talked. This seemed more comfortable for both of us.

Further, I conversed, "So, you are a former Marine."

"No, I am a Marine. Once a Marine, always a Marine," he said proudly.

I had noticed that his stance was most often with his legs apart, reminding me that he was truly a real man, a real Marine, masculine to the core. I liked this very much.

Robin or Chris would make spontaneous appearances. Did we want coffee? We chose to go to the kitchen table and Robin served us there.

After much talk about his family and his past years, my family and my past years, he asked if I would like him to bring some albums over on his return visit. This way I could acquaint myself with his family. (He planned to return; this pleased me.) How about the next day, he asked? To this, I extended the time almost a week, explaining that I had some household duties. I told him I was slow because of my inability to "navigate" without a walker or a cane and, therefore, it took me many more hours to accomplish a task than in years past. (From my response he knew he was extremely welcome.)

I saw him to the door and shook his hand. Though we had wrought iron railing, he was a little awkward in descending the few steps to the landing and the two steps to the driveway. This, too, was a problem of mine. We seemed to have so much in common.

"Mother, how did you like him?" Robin questioned after he drove away.

"Fine... Now, he is coming back in my memory. He was extremely handsome. In school, I can only remember him in one place. That was always in the library with an arm slung across the back of a chair or arms crossed on the table. He had black hair and dark skin." I stammered on, "Extremely quiet and shy.... well behaved... but oh, my... was he ever good-looking!"

Later, I was to learn that when she and Chris went to the other part of the house, she began to cry.

"What is the matter?" Chris asked. "I have lost my mother," she wailed.

"Robin, you're absolutely crazy. We couldn't get her out of this house for any man." He failed to believe her. He thought she was overreacting.

Marvin brought over two albums of photos of his family. They were most interesting and gave me an insight into how his life for more than half a century had been spent. He was definitely a devoted family man. In my mental estimation, it made him a remarkable man.

My family delighted in teasing me about him. They spread the word that, "Mom has a real live boyfriend... after all these years, she caught one."

Each time he came, he brought different albums for me to see. It was as if he wanted me to have something of him until he could return again.

Thereafter, when he departed from a visit, I would present my cheek for a kiss. When the girls heard about him returning so often, they asked, "Has he kissed you yet?"

"Yes, on the cheek when he leaves."

The response was, "That's no good, Mom, you need to let him know you like him!"

During the next visit, he often stroked my hands. At the door, when he departed, I suppose it startled him that I closed my eyes and waited for a kiss. His kiss was soft, as if he wanted to linger. That kiss made me feel like a young girl again.

My evaluation of him became more intense. This marvelous man was a war veteran, walking as if on stilts (and never complaining), had been married to the same woman for 52 years, had held a job for 30 years after his legs were lost, was by Helen's side for the last seven years of her fatal illness and would not put her in a nursing home, and, unless asked, did not reveal that he had lost so much for our country.

Weeks later, he showed me a TV sports feature tape of an interview by Hope Hines. Hope was a sportscaster and had played golf with Marvin, not knowing that he wore prostheses. This fascinated Hope when, by accident, he found out. He asked if he could do a special segment, showing Marvin swinging the golf club, driving his golf cart and doing his "usual thing" around the golf course. To be sure, it must have fascinated the viewers.

Marvin laughingly spoke of how one day he slipped on a wet exit at the golf course and took a spill. He did not feel that his leg had twisted in the prosthesis when he fell. To the horror of stunned fellow players who did not know his history, this loosened leg fell off as he stepped into his golf cart at the second hole. They wanted to stop the game and take him home. He would not hear of it. "I didn't want to ruin their game. I wanted to be useful, so I drove the cart around and kept the score for them." When the game was finished, someone drove him home, and the next day he ordered a replacement for the broken pin that fitted into his "stump" sleeve.

Without apprehension or hesitation, he talked freely about anything or any subject I chose. It was marvelous to converse with him. I didn't have to build a wall or be afraid that I was saying the wrong thing. We seemed to understand each other completely. Everything we did, no matter how trivial, seemed interesting and unique. I was so comfortable with him. He was like a new revelation to me... something I never felt before. It was as though I had known him all my life.

When Robin and Chris went to Colorado for their yearly visit, I kept the dog. Lady had been with us since she was a pup. She was a large, long-haired, black, mixed-breed mutt that all liked. Because of my fear of falling over her, my attention was confined to being sure she was let out to the fenced backyard and her comforts were secure, but petting and stroking were out. She knew of my affection for her and seemed to sense my desire to keep my distance, for safety's sake. She was always glad to see me and I, her, but we had a "mutual understanding" about distance from each other.

When Marvin would hesitate at the front door to kiss me upon departure, she would take a dash through the small opening in the door right out into the street. Fortunately, it was a cul-de-sac and she could only go the block's length. Marvin would have to go out and retrieve her. At first, he went to the end of the drive and tried to get her back by whistling and calling, but to no avail. This happened several times. The only solution would be for me to get a dog biscuit treat for him, in order to woo her back. When she returned for the biscuit, he would secure her dog collar with a leash and bring her in for me. He never once complained.

He asked me to accompany him to a reunion of veterans in Franklin, a town nearby. Because he understood my walker was cumbersome, Marvin suggested that he push me in his wheelchair. Stunned that he should be so very considerate and go to all of that inconvenience, my answer was affirmative. This man was indeed beyond gallant, he was unbelievable.

At the luncheon, he sat next to me and often held my hand under the table.

In the car, he took my hand and kept holding it as we rode along. "Marvin, aren't we coming to a two-hand corner?" At that, he reluctantly let go and put both hands on the wheel. This amused us when I would say this.

The car was a van, complete with controls that could be operated by hand. He preferred, whenever possible, to drive with his "feet" (prostheses), another feat that amazed me.

A few days later, he asked if lunch would be alright so that I could meet his daughter and grandson. We went to Margit's smorgasbord. Sherrie was very attractive, most charming, reminded me very much of her mother, as I remembered her. The grandson, Jason, was post-college, quiet, extremely likable, with features like his mother's.

At one point, Margit came to the table and spoke softly into Marvin's ear (but I overheard part of it)—"Looks like something could come from this."—or something to that effect. He smiled, nodding his head in agreement.

After the lunch, he asked if we could drive by his home. It was only a short distance from Margit's smorgasbord restaurant and her residence. (She built her own business after leaving the previous site, which was several blocks away on the same road. This had pleased me so much, at last to see her own her building as well as the business.)

Because of living on the other side of town, my visits to the smorgasbord were limited to maybe once a year. She was so happy that we had chosen our special day to be with her and told us so, as we departed.

Marvin pointed out his street as we approached his home. We entered a curved street with the lushness of countless overhanging green trees. The homes were modest on each side. Within a block, we passed through a stoned entrance. He indicated that the corner home was his and that he was the first to build in the small secluded area some few years before.

The four of us drove by, turning the corner by his home into a cul-de-sac street. At the end he turned and came back, approaching the house from the back side. I noted that it was a comfortable Ranch-style brick home, well-kept. My eyes fell on the slope and there, amid plants that were graduated to bloom all season, was a single stalk of corn. It stood bold and obvious.

Laughingly, he explained that one of the birds apparently left the seed. He found it entertaining to watch it grow, knowing that it would startle and amuse passersby because of its location. I chuckled in agreement, and encouraged him to leave it there.

I was puzzled that he should bring me by his home and more so, when he asked, "Would you like to go inside?"

"Oh no, perhaps another time," was my reply.

On one of our drives, he took me down Natchez Trace, then over to Columbia and Franklin to see the places where he lived as a child, before his family moved to Nashville. His mother had been a housewife, seeing to the garden and family while his father maintained the Military Academy building. He did the electrical work, as well as the plumbing and Marvin, at age 6, would go over and help his father sweep the furnace floor to keep it free of coal dust.

Additionally, Marvin helped his mother with the dishes and other mundane tasks. All this time my amusement grew, and my admiration for this man was overwhelming.

He told about his father working all the time, and his mother faithfully minding the house, eking out their vital needs by whatever means the Post-depression Times allowed her. The more he told me about her, the more her tenacity was obvious. To have known her would have been an honor.

His family consisted of two older brothers, an older sister, and a sister younger than he. On one day when he was about three years old, his brothers threw him in the well and tried to hang his sister. Alice, his mother, returned from laboring in the food garden just in time. Many times I teased him about that averted well tragedy and told him it occurred because it was apparent that he was the runt, insisting that he was his mother's favorite child, and the brothers were jealous. He denied all of this. It was a joy to tease him about anything.

During another outing, he took me by the church to which he was taken during his childhood. It was St. Peter's Episcopal Church of Columbia, Tennessee, established in 1827. Later, I was privileged to visit inside, to admire the architecture, furnishings and be dazzled by the stained-glass windows.

When he asked me to attend church with him on Sundays, my heart was warmed and grateful. For over 50 years, St. Philip's Episcopal had been his church. Eventually, I learned that he had made additions to the altar, had built and hung the holders for the church banners, had made the "reserved" pew signs (for special occasions), the announcement holders, built the library, made the holders that housed the mail for the individual church members and, with the help of his brother, had put the spotlight in the ground for the first sanctuary. Slowly, I extracted this information, knowing well that these were just some of the things built by his hands for St. Philip's. At these times, his shyness would show through, and it was difficult to get him to speak of them. To me, they proved his inner kindness toward others and his reverence for God.

My heart sang with joy every moment spent with him. He was truly delightful and so very genuine. In church, he sat as close as he could get, making sure his arm was next to mine. (Of all the churches in my past, this was the first Episcopal to attend.)

Oftimes, our conversations turned to our youth. He told me how he always ran everywhere, seldom ever walking. His legs were unusually strong. (This explained his ability to shinny up the palm trees to install communications during World War II.)

We talked about the old days, when he was about ten and I was seven. Living just blocks from each other, we went to the same neighborhood park, attended the same school but did not remember meeting except when he returned from World War II to complete his high school. He commented that my honors surpassed any of the classmates, so he knew about me from occasional school newspapers he received while in the service, and observing me when he returned to school. This pleased me to hear him say that he respected my past and knew me well. My response was that my memory of him was "that good-looking shy boy in the library." We dwelt for hours on our past, the people and the old neighborhood called North Nashville (Kalb Hollow or Germantown).

In subsequent conversations with him, I learned more about his youth and his military background. "I nearly drove Mom nuts, walking around the house singing, 'There's a Star-Spangled Banner Waving Somewhere,' as I hourly nagged her and Dad to sign for me to join the Marines. An uncle of mine was a Marine, and I wanted to be one, too. I was 17 and would have to register for the draft at age 18. I was only 5'5" tall, and my weight was 117. I was supposed to measure 5'6" and weigh at least 120 pounds. Anyway, after wearing them down, they went to sign for me. Two days later, I was on my way to San Diego."

He had been a Marine in World War II, serving in ground communications, came home safely, finished high school, took some extra schooling, went to work, married and had two children, Sherrie first, then Charlie.

When I pressed Marvin for more details than I learned at the North High reunion introduction about his Korean experience, he told me it had been difficult for him to speak of them. In the past, it seemed when people would ask, they did not seem genuinely interested. (I'm sure this was frustrating to him.) Apparently he clammed up, and I couldn't blame him. Eventually, this would change.

He received communications from a military friend, requesting his past experiences, especially in Korea. A book was being written, and he wanted to include Marvin's background.

After multiple contacts, Marvin succumbed to his wishes. One Saturday morning when Helen was shopping and he was home alone, he got a couple of beers and decided to speak of his whole experience in Korea, the place that took away his legs. (He promised to let me listen to the tape and read the subsequent transcript. I looked forward to this.)

My heart seemed to sing with every moment spent with him. Here we were in our early to mid-70s but feeling inside as if we were still half a century younger. My respect for him grew with each day that more was learned about him, and how he "ticked."

Laughter was a constant reaction, sometimes uncontrollable outright giggling from me. He made me so very happy. These unfamiliar new feelings, since meeting him, needed to be analyzed at home in my quiet moments, I mused...

"Did you know that I was a veterinarian doctor at one time?" He asked one day.

My mind skimmed over what he previously told me about his education. I knew he was an accountant and headed the credit union at his work. Perhaps he had taken some related courses and gone to school during the period between World War II and Korea. Somehow we turned to another topic, and it was forgotten at the time. Away from him, my curiosity grew as to why he did not pursue his training in that field of medicine. My plans were to have him elaborate on this.

When it was brought up again, he avoided the subject. Later, I learned why. He was building up my suspense.

"When were you a vet doctor, Marvin?" was my question, one day.

"Well, to tell you the truth, it was just for one day. My cousin, Clyde, and I were walking to school. We were in the first grade, as I recall. He told me their milk cow was sick. After school, I suggested that we look in on the cow. The poor old cow didn't seem to be faring very well and, when Clyde showed me the bottle of medicine, I suggested that she probably needed us to help her. The medicine wasn't doing her any good, because she hadn't been getting enough. I recommended that we give her enough to do a good job and make her well fast. He, too, thought it was the best thing to do for her, so I gave her the remaining doses, emptying the bottle. School, by now, had been over for some time, and I met my mother coming to see what was keeping me. I simply explained that we were looking in on Clyde's cow, but she should be all right now. The subject was dropped.

"The next morning I met with Clyde on the way to school, anxious to hear the cow was healed, but the news was bad. He said she died."

"What in the world happened to you two over this?" I gasped.

"I don't think they realized we had anything to do with what happened, and we did not volunteer anything. That was my first and last time to practice vet medicine. At the time, it seemed the right thing to do, but something went wrong, according to our thinking. We felt it was best not to mention our good intentions."

Following that, when he would suggest a remedy for something. I would tease him by saying, "Oh, yes, I forgot you practiced medicine."

Marvin would retort with a feigned expression of regret, but also a twinkle in his eye, "True, but my first and only patient died on me."

He often mentioned his children. I had met Sherrie, but not Charlie and David. Charlie had been with a grocery chain for almost 30 years. David had been with the Nashville Police Department, almost the same length of time. My initial meeting with David was unusual.

Marvin was taking me home on a humid summer evening after dark. We stopped at his local grocery to buy a special cereal that Robin wanted. He parked the van in line at the end of other customers' cars, but kept the motor running to give me the comfort of the air-conditioning. As soon as he was in the store's entrance, the van began to move forward very slowly. There was a large console that separated me from the controls, so reaching the brake was impossible.

What to do? Just don't panic! I could reach the keys. Right. That would stop the motor and the car. He will be returning within five minutes. Wrong on both counts. It kept creeping ahead, then it began to slowly roll backwards. I grabbed the steering wheel, driving to avoid hitting a pedestrian or another car. Traffic was always heavy on this street, and if the van continued this now reversed course downhill, I would end up in the middle of the busy intersection behind me. What to do? Steer the wheel toward the store's metal, support-roof posts on the entrance sidewalk, and pray they would stop the van. It hit the sidewalk, scraping the driver's side against the posts and grocery cart holder, and somehow stopped.

What to do now? Clerks and late shoppers hurried from the store, exuding with sincere kindness and concern, opened the door to be sure of my safety, then asked me to come inside and sit down, or what could they do for me? This seemed like a bad dream. I was so embarrassed, but humbly grateful that I was not hurt. Marvin's van was just a few months old, and it was now wrecked on his side. He hurried out of the store, pale and concerned that I could be hurt.

After checking to be sure that nothing had happened to me, he phoned his son, David, to come over. The police were called. David was off duty, lived nearby, and was there within five minutes. Shortly, a police car arrived, followed by another with a sergeant inside. Marvin introduced me to David. He calmly took over.

The rookie officer jested, "How do I write up an accident report for a car with no driver?" With a cane from the van and Marvin's arm for support on the other side, I walked the few steps to the officer's car to answer any questions he might have. There were none. The officers and David conversed, and Marvin drove me home.

On the way I said, "That was an unusual way to meet your son for the first time. He will probably tell you that

I could be a jinx to you, that this is an omen to drop that lady now.... You know, those people back there are probably saying I tried to make a drive-in store out of Hill's. How awful! Your beautiful car is wrecked."

He took my hand from across the console and patiently spoke, "I'm just grateful nothing happened to you. The car can be fixed. No problem at all. And, David won't say anything about the incident."

When we got to Robin's, I walked to his side of the van. I gasped at the damage, apologizing again and again. He calmed me by emphasizing that my welfare was more important to him than the van ever was and not to give the incident another thought. Inside the door, he kissed me goodnight, saying that he would phone. To assure me that he always got home safely, after dropping me off, he always phoned as soon as he got into his living room.

"Robin, if he never phones me again, I will understand. What a terrible thing. Even though it was not my fault, I still feel responsible since he left the car running for my comfort," was my explanation in describing the accident. "To top it all, this was my first introduction to his son, David. How awful!"

The phone rang the next day, and he explained that he had put the van in the repair shop. He put a rush on the repairs. "This is such an inconvenience for you," I moaned.

He answered by saying the car would be ready soon and not to be concerned. He phoned every day. Then in a short time, the van was back, and he picked me up the same day.

His kisses were many and welcomed. At every opportunity, he stroked my hands or my arm. "I love you," he repeated many times. To that, my reply was the same. One day in the living room without fanfare, he simply asked, "Will you marry me?"

Startled, I asked, "Will you give me two days for a reply?"

The next time he came, I told him that I would marry him. My mental checklist held nothing but respect and love for this man.

Indeed, I was deeply in love with Marvin.

In my rebuttal to his marriage proposal, I had asked him if he did not deserve and prefer a younger and healthier companion. He said he loved and wanted me. Only me. If I could accept his flaws, he could most certainly accept mine.

Robin got on the phone as soon as she learned, called her sisters first, and generally spread the word. As soon as anyone would hear, the question was almost always, "How is this possible when she never went anywhere to meet anyone?" or the usual comment "This assures me that it is never too late," or "Oh, there is a chance for me yet."

She was jubilant when she phoned Margit. "Are you sitting down? I have some wonderful news you will not believe about my mother." Robin said they were both crying throughout the conversation.

CHAPTER 17

It was now September. He wanted to set the date as soon as possible, joking that we were almost three quarters of a century old, which didn't leave us much time.

We wanted a simple wedding in St. Philip's Church, so that all who wanted to attend could do so. Thanksgiving was coming up, as well as Helen's yearly family reunion. This gathering was always on the first Saturday after Thanksgiving. He suggested we have the wedding before or after the reunion meal, as the reunion was always held on the lower level of the church.

"But what if the wedding guests mistakenly think that the reunion meal is the wedding reception? Thanksgiving is on Thursday, the reunion is on Saturday. How about having the wedding on Friday? Then, we could be home with our families for Thanksgiving, have the wedding on Friday, and be there for the reunion on Saturday. Then we attend church on Sunday morning, and leave for our honeymoon on Monday," I suggested.

"Great idea! I will see Peter (Father Whalen) and make the arrangements," Marvin replied happily.

An old school friend, Robert Burgess, was engaged to print the wedding invitations.

After several visits with Father Whalen for church-required premarital consultation, the date and time were firmly set. He was amused and delighted with our plans to marry.

Marvin asked that I go with him for the engagement ring, so the selection would be of my choice and preference. We went to the Green Hills area and chose a store owned by the same family for many decades. My choice was to remove two of the diamonds and replace them with our birth stones.

I was giddy with indescribable happiness. Imagine! At my age, selecting an engagement ring, a wedding dress, having alterations, buying wedding shoes, being pampered by him at every turn! Also, at every turn, he stroked my arms and hands, declaring his love for me. I was so in love with this man, that his presence overwhelmed me. He was indeed my treasure.

In the meantime, amid my blissfulness, 9/11 occurred. Marvin knew my deep feelings, my empathy for all of my fellow human beings. Therefore, he kept me busy, especially away from the television news. He deliberately consumed my time because he felt my grief would be too severe, thereby affecting my health. This consideration never occurred to me until a later time, when he confessed he was trying to protect me. (I was so intoxicated with his charm and attentiveness that every "fjord" was easier to pass through.)

Robin approached a newspaper reporter about our courtship and impending marriage. Sylvia Slaughter said a love story would be just the thing to help her readers bear the shock of 9/11. She phoned for an interview. She and Delores, the photographer, followed Marvin and me on one of our picnics, to rehearsal at the church, and as we sat in my home and at his home, in order to get details for the Tennessean.

The story appeared in the LIFE section and covered several pages with script and pictures from the different locales. The story was well told and caused positive response from the readers.

Our days were full. This had been a whirlwind courtship, beginning in July, though the first encounter was the June reunion. Now, we would be married on November 23.

One afternoon Marvin announced that we had to go get a marriage license, at Father Whalen's urging. On arrival at the municipal building, we had to walk a few short corridors. The last one, however, was unusually long (especially so, as my steps were slow with the walker). On reaching the door bearing the necessary title, we went in. There before us was a seated clerk. Her desk was flanked by what appeared to be two sets of parents of Oriental descent with apparent bride and groom-to-be answering questions, getting the same document we were seeking.

When the clerk looked up, the group turned to look at us, too.

"May I help you?" She asked, apparently sure that we had the wrong office.

"Yes," Marvin replied. "We want a marriage license."

The entire group softly chuckled and gave us amused glances.

"We were younger when we started down that hall out there," he quipped. With this statement, they burst into laughter.

Then, she seemed to hurry them through. Because she soon had us, too, out the door with proper document in hand.

"I guess the clerk thought we might not have much time left, so she rushed those youngsters through. And, us, too," he laughed.

Every day my love for him grew. His face was weather-beaten, with multiple deep wrinkles, but when he touched me and kissed me, they were insignificant, totally unimportant. The inside (the heart) of this precious man was the most important to me.

It didn't seem to matter that my experiences in kissing were "many years old." I explained that I always turned my cheek up to receive a kiss, even to my family. I returned their kisses in this manner. It seemed more "sanitary" and, too, I thought that kissing on the lips should be reserved for intimate moments with the man who might miraculously come along some day. When our lips met, the years faded and we were young again. Age didn't matter. I was lost in the ecstasy of his arms, off in another realm.

"You're everything I need to make me happy and to erase the loneliness I've known so long," he would say when we were alone. "I've been to some well-meaning meetings of singles, but I would come home, look at TV, fuss at the TV or the quietness of the house, and usually go right to bed only to wake early and start the same process of doing less.

"The first day I sat in Robin's living room with you, I knew I couldn't let you go. That day, I made up my mind that I would pursue you, no matter how long it took. You've made me happy again," he said, between kisses.

This made my heart sing. The warmth in my chest would surge and make me feel aglow and happy. How could these emotions be so intense? Why did I love him so much?

In rational moments, I felt I knew. He was loving, sincere, dependable, had the best of character and reputation, was a family man, was totally attentive to me—and didn't want to take me back to my home after a date. He would tarry as long as he could. I appeased both of us with the reminder that the wedding was not far off, and I then could stay with him for ever. He was always ready to lavish gifts (which I declined). Mine was a feeling of security, and being needed; and he told me never to mention again that a younger woman in better health would have been more appropriate for him. Most importantly, he had asked me to accompany him to his church. I could go on and on telling why I treasured him.

There was only one "blemish" in our relationship: He made me so happy that I could not help but giggle (yes, GIGGLE), sometimes aloud when we were alone, or muffled at inappropriate places. For example (how does one put this delicately?) at church. The first morning I attended church with him, we sat in the first pew, just behind where the lay readers sat. The printed program of the service was strange to me. I had worshiped in many different churches but, as mentioned, never the Episcopal church until now. There was a prayer book with Bible verses and appropriate quotations and prayers. The hymnal was divided into two parts. That meant that I had to look to him for a cue as to when to sit or stand (kneeling was out of the question for both of us), follow the printed order of service for hymns, responses, in order to keep up.

His singing was undoubtedly the worst I had ever heard from anyone before. This was amusing to me, and I tried so very hard not to show it, remembering that I was in church. The next time we stood, I deliberately did not share his hymnal with him, so that I could turn away from him a little as we sang. My musical knowledge was not excessive, but I could recognize a really bad singing voice when I heard it.

That morning, when his voice did a trill, I could not contain myself. It was absolutely too much. My shoulders began to shake from suppressing my uncontrollable urge to laugh. I looked up at the crucifix and dug my nails into my clinched hands to divert my attention. To no avail. It was as though something was dosing me with indescribable joy. Then I felt the incontinence from the water pill taken for high blood pressure. Oh, how could this be? Though I was totally humiliated and embarrassed, I simply could not control myself.

Happy when the hymn was over, I sat down, trying my best to look normal and composed. (Even when my children were young, I was sure they would not have lost their composure as I did in church.) We exited the side entrance and, as a result, we saw Father Whalen briefly. I profusely apologized, confessing that I had laughed through the service at Marvin's singing, but hoped that

I did not distract him from his sermon and other duties. Would he please forgive my rudeness?

This man who had the personality and round face (a ruddy complexion, white hair and white short beard, and serene personality), all the characteristics of Santa Claus, broke into a a broad smile and chuckled, "If you cannot laugh in church, then where else can you truly laugh?" He put me at ease. I sighed with relief. This endeared him more to me and made me aware of his gentle and kind nature, truly a man of God.

In the pew, not waiting for Marvin to help me, I hastily put on my coat, afraid my water pill "accident" was showing; however, it wasn't. Once in the car, I blurted out to Marvin about my accident and asked his forgiveness.

Tenderly, he took my hand and said, "Sweetheart, that doesn't change my feelings for you in any way. About my singing," he chortled, "Helen used to keep my ribs sore from punching me.... We will go by my house and I'll give you one of my robes to wear while I dry your clothes."

"But what if some of your family comes in while I'm in your robe? What would they think of me?"

He downplayed my objections, saying it would not matter. Sure enough, no one came in until long after he brought my dried clothes to me in the bathroom.

This episode and his nonchalant attitude made me love him even more, as if that could even be possible. No one ever knew of the incident. It was one we shared alone many times, laughing at my humiliation.

CHAPTER 18

One day on questioning Marvin about his service in Korea, he gave me a typed copy of the experiences he had related on the tape that Saturday morning several years before.

We had no date for the following day. That night I propped myself up in my bed, planning to read a few pages of his Korean War narrative and to finish it the next day or so.

No way. The more I read, the more I was mesmerized by the story's contents. Interruptions were out of the question. I was so spellbound, I could not lay it down until I read the last word on the last page. This man surely had "nine lives!"

He detailed the events, leaving me with astonishment that one man could survive all of this. I hugged the script to my chest and openly wept. It was titled "Defying Fate In Hell Fire Valley." This is what he wrote:

I was a corporal in the Marine Corps Reserve company in Nashville, Tennessee and a veteran of World War II when the North Korean Armed Forces invaded the Republic of South Korea on June 25, 1950. I was living in Nashville with my wife, Helen, our 25 month-old daughter, Sherrie, and our one-month-old son, Charles.

The reserve company that my brother, Jack, and I were assigned to was called to active duty on August 1st. This unit was transported to Camp Pendleton, California by train on August 21st.

Upon our arrival, our company was assigned to a Casual Unit for processing and individual reassignment based on our MOS (military occupational specialty). I was assigned to the Item (I) Battery, 3rd Battalion, 11th Marine Regiment, 1st Marine Division—an artillery unit. Jack was assigned to Fox (F) Company, 2nd Battalion, 7th Marine Regiment, 1st Marine Division, as a machine gunner in the machine gun section.

I, along with approximately 2000 other Marines, boarded the Navy troop transport, the USS Okanogan on September 1st. Just before sunset, on a clear afternoon, we embarked from the San Diego port. Jack sailed on the USS Bayfield the same day.

Approximately two and a half weeks after leaving the states, we docked at Kobe, Japan for six hours. While tied up at Kobe, I was able to visit with Jack for a short while. We did not see each other again, until I returned home some 13 months later.

On September 21st, we landed at Inchon, South Korea, just 31 days after leaving Nashville. Our mission was to reinforce the 3rd and 5th Marine Regiments, which had invaded and secured Inchon on September 16th.

While on board ship, I had been reassigned to an artillery F.O. (forward observer) team and attached to Baker

(B) Company, 1st Battalion, 7th Marine Regiment. After landing, this unit participated in the action east of Seoul and advanced northeast as the point unit to Uijongbu.

On October the 1st, the U. S. Army 1st Calvary Division moved through our established position, relieving us to return to Inchon. On October 3rd, we boarded LSTs (landing ship tank) and sailed up the East Coast of North Korea for an amphibious landing at the port of Wonsan.

Instead of a quick redeployment, we sailed back and forth off the coast of North Korea for almost two weeks. The reason for the extended sea deployment was that Navy mine sweepers were clearing mines from the waters off Wonsan.

When we finally landed, we were greeted with a large sign reading, "Bob Hope welcomes the 1st Marine Division." (While we had been on our extended "sea cruise," allied units had advanced up the coast to Wonsan and had been entertained by the USO show featuring Bob Hope.)

We moved north to the town of Hamhung and, on November 1st, I was reassigned to Item Battery. I served in Item Battery during the offensive drive deeper into North Korea, through the villages of Koto-ri and Hagaru-ri, to a position just south of Toktong Pass.

November 25th, two days after Thanksgiving, I was in the chow line for our delayed Thanksgiving dinner. The Battery Clerk walked up and told me to get my gear together, that my hardship discharge had been approved and that I was to hop a ride on the mail Jeep and return to Hagaru-ri. I left the chow line, returned to my tent, got my gear, but by the time I reported to the Battery

CP (Command Post), I was told that I had missed the mail Jeep by five minutes. I returned my gear to the tent and went back to the mess tent. The chow line had been secured. Not only had I missed my ride, I had also missed Thanksgiving dinner.

After morning mess on November 26th, we received orders to prepare to move out. We struck our tents, loaded the trucks, hooked up the 105 Howitzers and proceeded to a small village west of the Chosin Reservoir named Yudam-ni. This was the most northern point, reached by the 1st Marine Division, during the Korean "police action." I hadn't heard anymore on my returning to Hagaru-ri, so I continued my Battery duties.

There were some small arms fire in the hills that night. I would later learn that it was probing fire by an overwhelming force.

The next morning I was again told to report to the Battery CP for transport to Hagaru-ri. From there I was to proceed to Hamhung where I would be out-processed for return to the states. I was also told that if everything went well, I would be home for Christmas. I decided not to take my winter gear south with me, since I thought I could endure the 70 mile trip to Hamhung.

Once I was out-processed, I expected to be on a ship headed for the states in a couple of days. I gave my parka, snow packs, mittens, helmet, and everything else I didn't think I would need to my buddies in Item (I) Battery. I also left my rifle with the Battery since I was going to travel light, with only a change of clothing in my knapsack, dungaree jacket, cap and field jacket.

I was also carrying a few letters, some cash, and rolls of film that some of the guys had asked me to mail to their families when I reached the states. Our sea bags had been warehoused in Inchon back in September, so I didn't expect to ever see mine again.

About nine o'clock that morning, I left Yudam-ni in a Jeep to go back to Hagaru-ri with Captain Read, C.O. of How (H) Battery, along with his driver and Corporal David Berger from Headquarters Battery. During the trip back to Hagaru-ri, I learned that Corporal Berger was going stateside to attend OCS (Officers Candidate School) at Quantico, Virginia and that we would be traveling stateside together. I also learned that Captain Read had been in Yudam-ni scouting for a position to move How Battery from Hagaru-Ri to the Yudam-ni area.

It took most all day to travel the 14 miles to Hagaru-ri, because of the icy road. Dave and I were dropped off at the 11th Marine Headquarters. We were informed that we would spend the night there, and leave the next morning with a supply convoy that would take us to Hamhung.

That night, unbeknownst to us, the Chinese Army attacked the Marine troops in force at Yudam-ni, changing the plans and lives of the members of the 1st Marine Division as well as those of all the allied forces in Korea. It was recorded in the book, CHOSIN, written by Eric Hammel, that Captain Read's Jeep was the last vehicle to safely make the trip over Toktong Pass prior to this pass being blocked by Chinese troops.

Early in the morning of November 28th as we prepared to continue our trip, dark gray clouds hung low overhead and the temperature hovered around 30° below zero. The ground was frozen solid, covered with patches of surface ice and snow.

David and I boarded the convoy for Koto-ri, and it moved out. Shortly thereafter, we were halted at an MP traffic checkpoint near How Battery, located just west of a place called East Hill. We were told that a Jeep, traveling from Koto-ri had been fired on a couple of miles south of Hagaru-ri just before daylight, but had made it into Hagaru-ri safely.

We were then told that a recon team would scout the troubled area, and that we would have to wait for an "all clear" before moving on. Shortly, the recon team that was traveling in an open vehicle passed by us and traveled down the road about a mile. We watched as they turned east off the MSR (main supply route) and headed toward the ridge line, and finally south out of sight.

While waiting for the all clear, Dave and I talked with the fellows we would be traveling with, as well as a friend of mine from the Nashville Reserve Company, Wayne Frost, who had come over from How Battery to say goodbye. The men were concerned that I was traveling without winter gear, until I told them I would be going stateside soon after I got to Hungnam. Wayne asked if I would call his wife when I reached home, to let her know that despite the freezing conditions, he was well and that he still hoped to be home for Christmas. (On November 24th, General MacArthur had announced his "Home For Christmas" offense.).

The convoy consisted of three trucks and a Jeep. One truck led the convoy, followed by the Jeep with the remaining trucks bringing up the rear. Because of my light clothing, Berger insisted that I ride in the lead truck, which had a closed cab and heater, and that he would ride in the open Jeep. I was awfully glad to accept his offer because of the freezing temperature.

There would be two enlisted Marines and two South Korean officers riding in the bed of the lead truck. The Marines were part of a work detail going to load supplies and ammo at Koto-ri to bring back to Hagaru-ri. The Korean officers were returning to South Korea on leave.

After approximately 15 minutes, the MP received the "all clear" on his radio. I climbed into the truck. As it began to move, I looked back and saw Wayne standing on the side of the road. We looked at each other and, with a wave, we exchanged our farewell. I was on my way to Koto-ri. This simple gesture of goodbye to my friend on that long-ago freezing November day in North Korea also denotes the time and place I said goodbye to the life I had known for the past 25 years.

There was a farmhouse on the right side of the road where the recon vehicle had turned off the MSR (Main Supply Route). Several Koreans were standing in front of the house, waving their arms, as we drove past. I thought they were trying to stop us. I told the driver that they were trying to stop us for some reason, but he said, "Pay them no mind! They don't know anything we care to hear." We continued down the road toward an area that would later be named, "Hell Fire Valley."

We drove on to where the road turned sharply to the right. Just as we approached the curve, we could hear small arms fire in the distance. Thinking it was the recon team shooting at someone ahead of us, we took the curve at a safe speed. Or at least, it started that way.

Midway into the wide curve was a machine gun mounted on a stand and manned by a crew of Chinese regulars. The machine gun opened up on us, and the windshield disappeared. The driver floor-boarded the gas pedal and headed straight for the gun and its crew. I heard the gun clanging under the truck. When I looked back, I could not see any of the Chinese troops standing. I was sure that we had run over all of them.

We continued down the icy road toward Koto-ri, feeling sure that we had taken out the only trouble spot that we would encounter. I looked back a couple of times to see if any of the other convoy vehicles were following us, but the road was clear as far back as I could see.

(Thirty five years later, I learned that David Berger and the rest of the convoy had in fact stopped at the farmhouse where the Koreans had warned them about the impending ambush. They returned to Hagaru-ri and, later that day, Berger was transported to Hungnam by air.)

Turning back to the front, I saw that there were Chinese soldiers on both sides of the road ahead of us. It was too late to turn back. We had to try to run through the gauntlet of fire they had set up for us. The truck driver pointed to his carbine, which was in a rack above the windshield. I took it down and tried to pull the bolt back to chamber a round, but it was frozen.

By the time we had reached the enemy, it seemed they were all firing Thompson submachine guns at us. I put the butt of the carbine on the floor and used my foot to break the bolt loose and got a round loaded. Before I could fire, we had cleared the first group of soldiers, but I could see more of them ahead of us.

The driver said, "There are two hand grenades in the glove compartment." I reached to open the panel, but found it was locked. The keys were in the ignition. I picked up the carbine and fired as we entered the next group of soldiers; however, I couldn't see if I had hit anyone as we sped past them. The soldiers continued to fire at us with rifles and Thompsons. Some of them were tossing hand grenades at the truck. I tried to fire again, but the bolt was jammed with the spent casing. I used the heel of my hand to close the bolt to reload the casing and my foot to eject it. Some rounds would not seat properly when I attempted to close the bolt; the rounds would fall out. I was able to get off only five or six rounds from the first clip. There were two more clips in the ammo pouch on the stock of the carbine. When I inserted the second clip, I had the same problems. I was able to get about half of those rounds off, still not knowing if I had scored any hits.

Sometime during the running firefight, I had received a flesh wound in my left thigh, the only evidence being a little blood on my trouser leg. The truck driver had not been hit at all. We had been extremely lucky, considering the number of rounds fired at us, and the fact it was beginning to look like we would never run out of enemy troops.

We talked about another traffic checkpoint, that was about midway between Hagaru-ri and Koto-ri. By rough estimates, we figured we should reach it soon. Our thoughts were that surely the Marines still held that position, and we would reach safety. A little farther down the road, all of our hopes of reaching help vanished. The truck was slowing down to a crawl. The way we were bouncing, I knew that the tires were blown out. The engine sputtered badly, then died.

The driver said, "Look!"

I turned toward him. He was spinning the steering wheel like a toy top. Luckily the engine had quit when it did, because we were entering another curve and the truck went off the right side of the road. It nosed into a ditch which was deep enough to stop us. A few feet beyond the ditch there was a drop-off of about six feet to the bed of a river.

The driver yelled, "Tell the men in the back of the truck to bail out!"

When I turned to tell them we have to hit the ground, all I could see was mangled bodies. Blood was everywhere. The canvas cover was in shreds, blowing in the icy wind. I still held the carbine and had already loaded the third and last clip by this time. I jumped out the passenger door as the driver opened his door and jumped from the truck.

I went over the embankment and ran across a sandy area toward the frozen river, which was about 20 yards away. I looked back for the driver, and saw that he was just coming over the edge of the embankment. As I ran onto the ice of the frozen river, suddenly I was face down on the ice.

Struggling to get up when the driver reached me, I realized I could not bring my right leg under me to stand. I glanced back and saw that my right foot was turned backwards. Then I saw blood on my trouser leg above my right knee, where I had been hit again.

The driver skidded to a stop to help me and tried to lift me up. I knew I couldn't stand, and he would be unable to carry me any distance.

"My leg is broken, leave me here, and see if you can get away and send help back!"

We heard small arms fire behind us and looked in the direction of the truck. There, four Chinese were standing by the side of the road firing at us. The driver tried once more to pick me up. And I again told him, "Leave me! Try to save yourself!"

I handed him the carbine, pushing him away at the same time. Reluctantly, he left and ran up over the opposite boulder-covered riverbank and out of sight. The four Chinese ran past me in pursuit of him. Shortly, I heard heavy gunfire from that direction. I figured the Chinese had overtaken him and, if they had, he surely had not survived.

I slid over to the bank that the driver had crossed and had my body partially off of the ice, just as the Chinese came back over the rise. The Chinese talked among themselves for a short while, then walked back to the disabled truck.

They began looting it, taking everything they could use. I could see them stripping the bodies of the dead men. They took my knapsack, which contained the letters, film, and money that I was bringing out for my friends.

When they left the truck, three of them walked up the road to the north and one came in my direction. As I lay there, I realized I was numbed by the cold. I had not felt any pain when I was shot or when I had fallen, although my foot was turned completely backwards.

I was unable to see the Chinese, because he was standing behind me. But I heard the metallic click as he chambered a round, preparing to fire point-blank into me. After a poke in the back of my left knee, the leg jerked slightly and I knew he had shot me again. The guy fired his Thompson submachine gun in a short burst of probably 10 to 15 rounds. I could feel pokes all the way up my back. My body flinched with each poking sensation. I didn't feel the pain one would expect, but I thought I was fatally wounded because of the number of times I had been hit. At that moment my little daughter's face flashed in my mind, and I asked God to watch over my family.

When he stopped firing, he laid his weapon down and roughly turned me over on my back. He emptied my pockets, taking everything except a loose deck of well-used playing cards. These, he placed face down on a rock by my face. He took my wedding band and watch, then pulled roughly at my shoe laces, either trying to get my dog tags that were attached to them, or remove my field shoes. The laces would not give, so he let them drop.

He stripped off my field jacket, dungaree jacket and cap. When he pulled my undershirt up to remove it, I resisted at that. I reached up and pulled the shirt back down. He pulled the shirt up again and I, again, pulled it down. If he got that shirt, I would have no clothing above the waist. He gave me a dismissive look and walked away, leaving me alone on the ice.

I felt over my back in an effort to determine the number of wounds I had received there. When I found no blood on the places where I thought there should have been wounds, I wondered what all those pokes were that I had felt earlier. I knew then that God had spared me sudden death, and I asked Him for the strength to continue to fight for survival. There I lay on that rocky frozen riverbank, my right leg broken, my left thigh and knee shot through, and most of my clothing taken. The temperature was around -30° and dropping as nightfall approached.

Heavy gray clouds were still overhead and a brisk north wind was blowing down through the valley. I lay there trying to think of some way I might get back to our lines. I turned my head to one side and there lay the deck of cards I had forgotten about. It looked like they were still all there, since I couldn't see any that had blown off the stack. I looked at the deck of cards several times. I had a "premonition" what the top card was, and wondered if I was correct. Finally, I got the nerve to reach over and pick it up, and wasn't surprised to see the ace of spades. I slowly placed the card back on the deck. That deck of cards laying open to the wind has been recalled to my mind many times since last I saw them.

Thoughts of my wife and children waiting for me at home gave me hope and strengthened my desire to survive, and reinforced the possibility that I might still make it home for Christmas. I knew that any progress toward that goal had to start with me. Looking around for anything to splint my leg, I thought if I could stabilize it there might be a chance. I could slide along the iced-over river and return to Hagaru-ri.

The bank of the river that I was on was covered with rocks, while the opposite bank that I had run across earlier was sandy. As I thought of the difference between the two banks, it came to me that if I could get to the other side, I might be able to scoop out a hole, large enough for me to get into and be below ground level, and out of the freezing wind.

I lifted my right leg below the knee and crossed it over my left shin. It worked pretty well. I was able to scoot on the ice backwards, crossing the river and up on the sand several feet from the edge of the frozen river. The sand was not frozen solid, since there was little moisture in it.

I began scooping sand with my hands until I had a body-size depression. Then by pushing sand back to the edges from the surrounding area, I was able to double the depth of my shelter that would protect me from the wind. I moved around, until my body lined up with the depression. Then, gritting my teeth, I rolled into my little life-saving foxhole.

When my body settled on the bottom of the depression, I sat up and straightened my leg, then lay back flat, still only inches below the lip of the sand I had piled up. I looked at the heavy clouds overhead. Darkness was fast approaching, and snow was in the air. I was out of the wind and did not feel any pain from the cold or my wounds. My strong will to survive sustained me; I was beginning to feel peaceful. Darkness soon surrounded me as my first day in "Hell Fire Valley" ended.

Upon waking the next morning, November 29th, and opening my eyes, all I could see was what seemed to be a heavy fog. Blinking my eyes didn't help. Fearing that the loss of blood or the severe cold had somehow affected my eyesight, I reached up to rub my eyes to try and clear them. To my surprise, I brushed away about eight inches of snow, renewing my vision. The snow had fallen during the night completely covering me and insulating me from the cold air above. The sun was shining brightly and, with the new day, my will to live strengthened. I knew that with God's help, I would make it through another day.

Not long after waking up, I saw a man walking along the road. He was not in a uniform, so I assumed he was a civilian. I called out to him. He stopped and looked at me. I motioned for him to come down to where I was, but he just stood there and stared at me for a moment. Then he turned and walked away to the north. This was a good indication to me that there were Chinese still in the area and he was probably afraid to come to my aid. I knew he was only trying to survive the same as I.

Later that day, I heard small arms fire in the distance; it seemed to be south of my position. As time passed, the noise of the firefights were coming closer to me. I began thinking that my prayers would soon be answered and a rescue party was on the way.

As I looked south along the road, forms began to take shape as they ascended a hill on the east side of the MSR (Main Supply Route). The firing was quite heavy as they pursued the Chinese up the slope. They reached the crest and continued firing for several minutes. Then they turned and began descending the hill.

Once more, firing started on the crest. The Chinese had again occupied the hilltop and were firing on the American troops as they went down the slope. I watched as this up and down exchange was carried out several times. Then I heard the engines of vehicles coming in my direction, which turned out to be an American convoy, transporting the troops that were firing at the Chinese.

My position was about 20 yards from the embankment that we had descended when we left the truck the previous day. The road was several feet away from the embankment. From my angle of sight, I could see the turrets of two tanks which were spearheading the convoy as it approached. When I could see the tank commanders, I began yelling at them, but they couldn't hear above the noise of their vehicles. They passed on to the north.

A number of trucks rolled by, still no one heard my calls for help. My spirit began to sink when I realized that they weren't searching for me. They were moving to Hagaru-ri, and I was being overlooked.

After many more vehicles had passed, the convoy suddenly came to a stop. As the engines idled, I began yelling as loudly as I could, hoping to attract someone's attention before the convoy started moving again.

A firefight had broken out on the east side of the road. The noise from this action made it difficult for anyone to hear me, but I continued to yell.

Soon, a man walked to the edge of the embankment and barked, "Who the hell is doing all of that yelling?"

"I'm an American Marine, and both my legs are broken. I need help."

He disappeared from sight. Shortly, four men came over the bank and headed down to me. They brought a large canvas with them, asked about my injuries, and gave me a quick lookover. Then they carefully placed me on the canvas. With a man at each corner, they carried me up to the road.

I was placed in a trailer attached to a Jeep. The trailer was filled to the rim with boxes of (frozen) C-rations. They covered me with the same canvas they had carried me on.

These troops were curious as to why I was there by myself. I told them about the other men that had been in the truck, and how we had tried to escape the ambush by the Chinese. Pointing to the disabled truck which was nearby, I told them of the bodies that were in it and about the driver, but none of them volunteered to go look for his body.

The firefight raged on. They made every effort to keep the Jeep and the trailer between them and the direction of the enemy fire. One fellow said, "Don't worry, Buddy! You'll be in a hospital tonight between clean white sheets, with plenty of heat and chow."

Someone asked if I wanted a shot of morphine. My reply was negative, and that I wasn't in any pain. (I had heard before that you should not take morphine unless it was absolutely necessary, because it would thin your blood and could cause your body to freeze faster.) Frankly, I thought that I was freezing fast enough.

Someone else suggested a shot of sick bay brandy. That sounded better. "Yeah, I'd like that," thinking that it might warm my insides a little and pep me up a bit. A medic was nearby and said he would go to the medical Jeep and bring one back. I never saw the medic again or my brandy. He most likely found more serious work to do, because the firefight was continuing.

As night approached, the convoy had not moved. The firing was still heavy. I drifted in and out of consciousness. All of a sudden, it was pitch black. The firing had increased, and the troops of the convoy were having a hard time. I could hear someone shouting orders and others calling for help. Then, I lost consciousness again.

When I awoke sometime later, the firefight had stopped. The convoy was not moving, and I could hear men calling for medics. I realized that we had been surrounded and possibly overrun.

Footsteps were crunching on the snow-covered road. They would stop momentarily, followed by a metallic sound, then an explosion. After hearing several of these repeated sound patterns, I realized someone was dropping hand grenades in the vehicles as he made his way down the line of Jeeps and trucks. As he got closer to my trailer, I was hoping that he would run out of grenades. But that was not to be.

I felt the canvas that covered me being lifted and heard the loud metallic sound as a grenade hit the trailer bottom. I heard the explosion and had the sensation that I was being lifted. It seemed like I was lifted several feet into the air. Fortunately for me, the grenade had fallen between the trailer side and the stacked boxes of C-rations. The boxes absorbed most of the explosive force and the grenade fragments, but the concussion knocked me out.

While unconscious, I had dreams that were extremely vivid. The images seemed so real. An enemy soldier talked to me in perfect English – an American that had been captured accompanied him. The enemy told me that he was a member of Philippine Communist guerrilla troops that had come to Korea to help drive the Americans out. He told me that the convoy had been captured. The seriously wounded would be left near the road and, if American medics came, we could be treated and moved to our lines.

The American told me that this was included in the terms of surrender and for me to hang on, because help would arrive sometime after daylight. These nightmares still haunt me. Were they really dreams, or did I truly talk to a Filipino guerrilla?

The next time I awoke was sometime after daylight on the morning of November 30th. I was lying on the metal bottom of the trailer and not on the C-rations boxes. Someone had stolen all of my C-rations while I had been asleep. The canvas was still over me, but it was frozen so stiff that it acted like a roof covering the trailer.

I sat up and pushed the canvas back so that I could look around the area. There were enemy soldiers everywhere. They were looting the bodies of the dead and the abandoned vehicles. After they carried away all the loot they could find, they began patrolling up and down the road.

There were five wounded Americans walking nearby. I called out to them. When they came over, they informed me that they were being allowed to walk out or find a serviceable vehicle in order to go to Koto-ri and send back medics to treat the wounded. The medics would be allowed to take the wounded out.

I asked for water, but all of their canteens were frozen. One of them did, however, hand me a 5-gallon can of water from the Jeep pulling the trailer I was in. It was also frozen solid.

The men found a Jeep in a ditch nearby. After some effort, the engine started and all of them piled into it. As they were trying to drive the Jeep out of the ditch, a lone enemy soldier came up on the far side of the road and fired a Burp gun at the men in the Jeep, killing all of them. I watched this slaughter in horror, then closed my eyes and turned away; for I could do nothing to help them. The Chinese had no intention of honoring the terms of the surrender. I knew my chances of rescue were greatly diminished.

I was getting really thirsty. There was no snow in the trailer for me to eat, and the dry snow that had fallen during the night had blown off the canvas. So I put the 5-gallon can on my chest, hoping my body heat would melt just enough for me to get a sip or two from it. I soon gave up when I realized my body heat would not melt the frozen water.

I lay there all day as Chinese soldiers patrolled up and down the road, alongside the vehicles. During the afternoon, a new group took over the watch.

Under the canvas, I lay with my head next to the Jeep and my feet at the rear of the trailer. The canvas that covered me was frozen so stiff it was like a thin sheet of wood, which prevented it from buckling or folding.

One of those new dudes amused himself by grabbing the corner of my canvas and pulling it off of me. As this guy would walk past me, he would grab the corner of the canvas and slide it down and off my body and drop it. Then he would keep on walking. The canvas would teeter, then rest partly on the trailer's edge and the ground. I'd rise up as he continued down the road and pull it back over me.

On all of his trips down the road, we continued this "game" until he went off his watch. He, at least, gave me something to focus on rather than just lying there freezing. Maybe that was his reason for doing it. I don't know.

But the more aggravated I became, the more determined I got. These actions strengthened my will to live.

Night was falling again, my third night in "Hell Fire Valley." My situation hadn't improved very much. I still remained within a few feet from where I had been wounded. I fell asleep, still thinking that a rescue attempt might be made to save the surviving members of the convoy.

Sometime during the night, I was awakened by two of the enemy soldiers who were pulling on me and motioning for me to get out of the trailer. I tried with hand signals to show them that both my legs were broken, but they didn't understand. They continued to motion for me to get out.

Eventually, they took me by the armpits, one on each side, and slid me over the side of the trailer. They stood me beside the trailer and, as soon as they released me, I crumbled to the ground. Finally, they realized that I could not stand, so they turned and walked away. I called out after them with some choice words for leaving me on the ground. At least in the trailer I was out of the wind.

A short time later, I heard footfalls approaching. Four Chinese appeared with a stretcher. They placed me on it, picked it up and started carrying me toward the north. After a short walk, they turned east off the road and across the railroad tracks. We went up a hill and, after several minutes, we reached the crest.

Since it was quite dark, I couldn't see much of the surrounding area, but I could hear a number of men talking in Chinese. The men carrying me stopped, took me off the stretcher, and placed me on the ground. They pulled me over on what felt like a straw covered surface, then walked away, leaving me in total darkness and all alone. I thought.

Startled by someone asking me in English if I was an American, I said, "Yes. I'm an American Marine. Who are you?" The voice replied, "I'm an American Marine also, and there are two other men here with me."

He said that one was a US Army soldier, and the other was a British Commando. Although I was unable to see any of them in the dark, it felt good to be around people I could talk with.

I learned that these three men had been with the convoy and had been captured after they were wounded. They told me that the Chinese had marched all of the ambulatory prisoners away to the north on the night of their capture.

The Marine told me that he was a member of a Military Police Company and the Army soldier was with the 3rd Infantry Division. The Commando said he was with the Royal Commandos under Colonel Drysdale, the commander of the task force that was moving to Hagaru-ri to reinforce the troops in that area.

Sometime after our bull session, I fell asleep, but it was short-lived. Someone was kicking my feet. A Chinese soldier leaned over and handed me a canteen cup that contained a hot liquid.

The Royal Commando said, "Take a swallow and pass it on!"

After my sip, I knew there would only be enough left for each of them to take a small swallow, so I passed it along to the next fellow. I couldn't see what the liquid looked like, nor could I smell or taste it. All I remember is when I took that swallow, I knew my prayers were being answered. I think I know how Moses felt when he received manna from heaven. The warmth from that one sip spread throughout my body. I soon fell asleep and wasn't disturbed anymore that night.

Awakened by the light of a new day (December 1st), I could see that I had been placed under a lean-to. It was open on three sides with the roof sloping almost to the ground in the rear.

The roof was a lattice made of rough strips of wood and covered with straw, most of which had been blown away. The roof was supported in the rear with three short posts, and in the front by poles about five feet high. Under the roof in the rear was a small supply of hay, probably meant for oxen that had been sheltered there. The earthen floor where we lay was partially covered with loose hay.

From where I lay, I could see that in the area to the front of the lean-to, the Chinese were manning machine guns and mortar positions. They had positioned them to cover the MSR (Main Supply Route) at the foot of the hill. There was a farmhouse about 50 yards to the south that they were using for sleeping and warming. Smoke was coming from the chimney.

During the day, I got better acquainted with my fellow captives. We must have exchanged names and home towns, but later I could not remember them. (Luckily, some 40 years later, I learned that the Royal Commando's name was Kenneth Williams from Shearing England. Kenneth and his lovely wife, "Sunshine," attended The

Chosin Few Reunion in New Orleans in 1992. My wife, Helen, and I celebrated a very special reunion with them. The Chosin Few is a fraternal organization. Membership is limited exclusively to personnel that served on the ground in the Chosin Reservoir area, as well as Airmen that dropped supplies and evacuated the wounded, and all support groups, including naval personnel on ships in the area. Unfortunately, the identity of the two other captives is still unknown to me.)

When the Chinese brought me up from the road, they had placed me under the front of the lean-to. Kenneth Williams was on my right side and the Army trooper on my left. The Marine MP was behind us toward the rear of the shelter. The Marine had two chest wounds, yet he was able to move around better than the rest of us. Williams had been wounded when a hand grenade exploded near him and the firing mechanism had lodged in his knee, which he had pulled out himself. The result being, he was immobilized like myself. I cannot recall the wounds that the Army soldier had suffered.

When Williams and the others were taken captive, the Chinese allowed them to keep their winter gear and sleeping bags. With these items they were bundled up quite well against the miserably cold temperatures.

The Marine MP removed the waterproof shell from his sleeping bag and passed it to me. Without it, I don't think I would have survived those bitter cold days. I was unable to get it over my feet, because I couldn't move my broken legs. After making a number of unsuccessful attempts to get into the shell, I eventually gave up and just laid it over my body. I tucked it around and under me the best I could and, at night, would cover my head with it. The Marine that shared this life-saving cover with me died on December 3rd.

Williams was lying under the north side of the lean-to, the side that received the most snowfall. The snow would pile up against him, and he would retrieve enough of it to help quench our thirst. He had found an empty C-ration can, which he would fill for us after every snowfall. Fortunately, it snowed almost every night.

I had kept track of the first few days after being wounded. I wanted to count the total number of days until what I believed would be our inevitable rescue. Looking forward to that day, I found a small stone that was near one of the posts and started scratching a mark on the post for each day we were there.

The Chinese moved about frequently to relieve the men manning the weapons positions, so they could go to the farmhouse and get warm. When they walked past us, we would bless them with some pretty rough language. We didn't know if they understood us or not. They would just grin as they walked by.

One night, one of the Chinese gave each of us three boiled grape-sized potatoes. This was the only solid food we received while there. Surprisingly, this Chinese spoke to us in broken English. He told us they had no medical supplies to treat our wounds. After that, we didn't swear at them when he was around.

Every day we watched airplanes flying overhead. Sometimes, we saw them dropping bombs and napalm on the hills to the north of us. We can only speculate as to what was happening since our capture. With as many enemy troops as there were on our hill, we knew it must be real bad at Hagaru-ri and beyond.

Our planes never fired, or dropped armaments on our hill. I believe someone knew we were there. The reason I think this, was because the Chinese made no effort to conceal themselves. Yet no offensive action was taken to remove them from our hill.

We could only hope and pray that help would arrive soon. My marks on the post were adding up to what I felt were unbelievable numbers. We were all surprised that we had survived for so many days without food and endured such cold weather. I can remember that sometime during those days of captivity we had talked over reunion in San Francisco after we were rescued, but now that possibility seemed remote.

One morning I woke to the sounds of vehicles moving along the MSR. A hill below our position blocked our view of the road. None of us could tell which directions the trucks were moving. We listened to the vehicles all day and could not figure out why the Chinese didn't react to them. It came to me there could be only one explanation, the Chinese vehicles were moving south. That meant that Hagaru-ri and Yudam-ni had been overrun, and the Chinese forces were advancing south. That had to be the reason that the Chinese were still going about their normal routine, as if nothing out of the ordinary was happening. Our hill seemed unchanged as night fell and the traffic continued on the road.

Another freezing December morning dawned. The sky was cloudy and several inches of new snow had fallen during the night. I began to realize that something was different. We thought we could still hear the activity down on the road, but it was quiet around us. There were no Chinese about; their machine guns and mortars were gone. We had heard nothing of their departure. The only answer I could imagine was that the troops that had been occupying our hill had joined the advancing Chinese forces in their movement to the south and had abandoned us.

With all hope of rescue gone and no possible way to escape due to our physical immobility, our morale plummeted, and to say we were dispirited was an understatement. According to the markings on my post calendar it had been only two days since we had experienced the cold dismal Christmas Day. Thinking of our hopeless situation, I gave thanks for being allowed to see one more Christmas. We talked of the long odds that we had beaten over the past 30 days and were awed by the miracle that we were still alive.

Suddenly I heard a crunching noise. It was coming from up the hill behind the lean-to and out of our line of sight. It was the unmistakable sound of someone walking on the frozen snow.

Shortly, a man appeared about 50 feet away going in the direction of the road below. I think we all said together, "That's a Marine!"

He had his rifle slung on his shoulder. We called out to him. He turned, quickly brought the rifle down and, in one fluid motion, had us covered. He was as shocked to see us as we were thankful to see him. When he realized he was in no danger from us, he walked over and asked, "What the hell are you guys doing here?"

We told him that three of us had leg wounds and a fourth man, a Marine, was dead.

We could see that he was also wounded in the left shoulder. He said that he was on his way to the road to get medical attention, explaining that the Chinese had surrounded the Marine and Army units, but had been unable to stop the withdrawal south toward Koto-ri. The vehicles we could hear were the Marine convoy moving south, and the convoy was being secured by troops clearing the ridges of enemy troops on both its flanks.

He told us when he reached the convoy, he would tell someone where we were.

After a short while eight Marines came running up the hill carrying four stretchers. They placed us on them and, as we were getting ready to leave the hill, I thought to ask one of them if he knew the date. I wanted to verify my post calendar. He looked at me and said, "Man, this is Pearl Harbor Day, December 7th." It was not December 27th, which my marks on the pole reflected.

On most days of our captivity the sky was filled with low hanging clouds and it had been difficult to determine the time of day. I must have mistakenly counted some days more than once, after falling asleep for short naps. Each time I awoke I thought I had slept a full night. The chance of me returning to the states before Christmas was still possible, since it was three weeks away.

When we reached the road, we were placed in trucks that were already overloaded with men and equipment. I don't think any of my fellow captives were placed in the truck with me. They loaded us as they found available space.

The truck they loaded me into had a lot of men in it. At first, I couldn't understand why they put my stretcher on top of them. My face was almost touching the top of the truck-bed's canvas covering.

As the truck began to move, I turned my head toward another Marine, thinking we could talk a little to pass the time. One look and I knew he was dead. I could hardly move, but looking at the men on the stretchers that I could see, I realized that they were all dead. Now I knew why I had been placed on top of all those other men. My trip with those dead comrades is one of the events that will forever be etched in my memory.

CHAPTER 19

When we arrived at the aid station at Koto-ri, I was taken to a warming tent. Kenneth Williams and the Army trooper were also there. I was again offered a shot of morphine, but I refused. The corpsman tagged us as casualties, describing our wounds on the tag he attached to our clothing. He also asked us if we were the captives that had been picked up. We told him that we were. Leaving the tent, the corpsman told us that we would be evacuated as soon as possible.

While lying there waiting, I began to think of how awful I must look. Several weeks without a shave, probably two months without a haircut, wearing very little clothing, and that was filthy. I hoped that he didn't think that I was an enemy soldier.

The corpsman returned sometime later with several syringes. This time we got the morphine shots, whether we wanted them or not. He explained that we would soon be flown out and they wanted to make sure we were comfortable.

Two men came in, picked up my stretcher and carried me outside to just behind the tent I had been in to where there was a hastily constructed airstrip. They placed me at the end of a long line of other stretchers.

Shortly a plane (probably a C47 cargo transport) landed and rolled up close to the tent. The door opened and men began loading the wounded at the other end of the row from me. They got to the guy next to me, loaded him on the plane and closed the door.

In a few minutes the plane revved up its engines, taxied to the end of the airstrip and took off. I thought they had forgotten me, since there was no one but me. I was left there by the side of the airstrip by myself for what seemed like a long time. No one came to tell me why I had been overlooked.

Then, a small single-engine plane landed and taxied up near me. Two men came out of the tent, opened the door in the side of the fuselage and slid me inside.

Two more wounded men were brought out of the tent and their stretchers were clamped under the wings, one on each side of the plane. I learned later that one of these men was Kenneth Williams. I think the other was the Army soldier. (I'm not sure, since I've never heard from him again.)

We rolled down the air strip and took off. As we flew south down the valley toward Hungnam, the plane was at such a low altitude that I could hear gunfire on the ground. We assumed they were shooting at us.

When we landed at Hungnam, I was taken to the docks and then transported to the USS Consolation, a Navy hospital ship. In a ward on board the hospital ship, a routine evening food tray was placed by my bed. I hungrily devoured the contents. This was a mistake. All the next day I was sick from putting so much food in a stomach that had been empty for so many days.

The following day, I was put in a body cast. It reached from armpits to my toes. This was done, I was told, to help straighten my broken legs from the bullet wounds (the bones were splintered by the impacts).

Days later, I was flown from the airport at Hungnam to the Naval Hospital at Yokosuka, Japan. I was there for several days, where I received treatment for malnutrition and dehydration. They administered penicillin for my infections and pneumonia that had developed. I had an allergic reaction to the penicillin, which required different medications. (For relief from the drug reaction, another Marine gave me a coat hanger for scratching inside the cast.) Again, good treatment was administered to stop the itching (and disposal of the coat hanger).

I also received successful treatment for my frost bitten fingers and hands. My feet and legs had been frozen to within a couple of inches below each knee. Gangrene had started in them as soon as they began to thaw.

One special nurse (from New Jersey) came to my bed daily and massaged my frost bitten hands. Surely, without this devoted attention, my fingers also would have been lost.

The Naval surgeon advised me that he would have to amputate my legs. On December 22, I was taken to the operating room. There, I was administered an anesthetic. I began to sleep, but soon woke to a sense of someone marking across my leg. It was the doctor drawing and explaining to his aides that he planned to amputate at the places he indicated, the right leg above the knee and the left, just below the knee. I objected, even though he explained that I would be returning for more amputation later. To this, I replied that I would take my chances. On waking, I was pleased to find that he had honored my wishes to spare my knees.

On Christmas Day, I celebrated the holiday in a warm hospital, not in the states as I had hoped, but at least I wasn't on the frozen ground in North Korea. Boxes of M&M candies were passed out to all of the patients on my ward. They were a tasty Christmas treat, a reminder of home.

On December 27, I was loaded on an Army evacuation airplane and flown to the United States.

On my way to the states, I mulled over parts of my life up to this point. My thoughts were often of my father's brother, Jack Jolly Pugh. Because he was a Marine, I idolized him. In World War I, he lost a lung to gas. In addition to the name Jack, he was affectionately known as the "Mississippi Gambler." His colorful reputation let it be known that the officers as well as the enlisted owed him money on payday.

I often thought of my mother, Alice. She, as most mothers, during World War II dreaded the draft notices that were sure to come for their sons. My older brothers, Jack (named after the "Mississippi Gambler") and Warren, were already in the military. Now I, the youngest son, wanted to serve. My mother and my dad finally relented and took me to sign up for the Marines.

Jack and I were called in from the Marine reserves, when the Korean conflict started. Within three days after he landed in Korea, Jack was severely wounded. A 120mm mortar shell exploded in front of his foxhole. The fellow Marine, Leon Whiteside, who was also severely wounded with Jack, had departed Nashville with us in the beginning. (We had been high school and neighborhood friends.)

Jack's misfortune allowed me to secure a hardship discharge three months later and, now, my journey home.

(One incident that happened in the Valley was the call for much-needed ammunition. The code word for the ammunition was Tootsie Roll. Instead of dropping ammunition, the Air Force dropped containers of the candy. This did not prove to be a disaster, because it supplied the men with much-needed food. From the time of the first reunion of the CHOSIN FEW, a VIP representative of the candy company has brought special-made Tootsie Rolls for all to enjoy.)

An Army Air Force evacuation plane flew me, along with the other wounded, from Japan to Guam, and then to Hawaii. During my day-and-a-half stay in the Naval Hospital, I was given the Purple Heart. Our next stopover was in Oakland, California. Before landing, the pilot circled twice to allow us time to feel and express the emotions of seeing HOME again.

After leaving the Naval Hospital there, we stopped at the Houston Army Hospital. Our last stop was the Philadelphia Naval Hospital where I was to recuperate for several months.

Shortly after my arrival at the hospital, my lovely wife, Helen, and my sister, Virginia, were reunited with me for a welcomed but emotional visit.

Another weekend, Helen brought my daughter, Sherrie Lynn. This was a joyous reunion filled with love. It, too, was a special romantic time for Helen and me. Our second son, David Richard, was born on November 13, 1951 of that year.

As I strengthened, mentally and physically, I joined in the recreation and entertainment provided us.

On one night we were to be guests of a local Philly Club. (How to get there? No problem.)

One of the patients had a car, but he was on crutches and had one leg missing. This guy also volunteered to push the row of wheel chairs.

However, when he was pushing us, he chose to leave his crutches in the car and hop. We lined up and each man pushed the other chair in front of him. We must have looked like an odd lot with the one pusher hopping on his one leg. The important thing was we made it back and forth to our destinations many times, to the amusement of the onlookers who saw us, stepped out of the way for us and cheered us on.

Two days before my discharge from the hospital, I was given "legs." I took several steps on a ramp that had a waist-high rail on each side for support. That was the extent of my physical therapy. I was medically retired from the Marine Corps on October 3, 1951. Finally, I was able to return to my home in Nashville, Tennessee.

CHAPTER 20

I put the manuscript close to my heart and pondered the insanity of war. How could man do these things to one another?

Marvin was only a boy (however, he keeps telling me that he was a MAN) when he entered the Marines at age 17. (His mother must have suffered greatly to give two of her children and later, three, to the wars.)

It was difficult to equate that gung-ho young Marine of the 1940s and 1950s with the peaceful man of 2001 that I planned to marry. I smiled at the comparison.

Two days later, I was at Marvin's home and told him I was moved by his horrific ordeals in Korea.

"Will you please show me your Purple Heart? I have only seen them in pictures before."

Marvin opened the armoire door and took a small box out. From it he placed the medal in my hands. I held it carefully, awed by its symbolism.

Gently, Marvin said, "This should go to you, too. You have earned a Purple Heart for all the battles you have experienced. Mine lasted a short time, but yours went on for many years."

His sincerity touched my emotions. How could this "ten-foot-tall man" say these wonderful things to me? In a few moments, after my admiring this medal of honor, his next words were: "You keep it!" Stunned by this unbelievable gesture, I objected and muttered, "No! No! This belongs to you and your family. I cannot accept such a gesture."

I don't know what his feelings were about my refusal, but I was sincere in my reason to refuse this immeasurable honor. Tears gently fell down my cheeks.

After many good-humored verbal opinions back and forth, I added, "Well, I guess we have a mutual admiration society going on here in this room." At this, he took me in his arms and my tears subsided.

The phone rang and Marvin picked it up. "Hello. It's for you." Then he gave me the phone. It was Robin. She said with humor in her voice, "Is this Useless or Worthless speaking?" She was referring to the fact that we were giving only scant help toward our forthcoming wedding. True, we were too infatuated with our new-found love for each other that we seemed to be constantly in a daze. (Robin later said we were in no daze. Our condition was heavier than the London Fog.)

She wanted to remind us to pick up a package at our local hardware store. I don't think we remembered, so Chris did it for us. At the beginning of our engagement, Marvin and I turned the wedding over to her. She was "in charge." However, she needed lots of help and, since we were not dependable, she had to ask others for aid or do it her self. Though she (lightly) complained, we knew this was pretense and was loving every moment of the duties.

It was decided that we would ask Robin to be my matron of honor and David to be Marvin's best man.

After a few meetings with Father Whalen, invitations went out.

To us, the coming wedding had the air of festival preparations akin to the Mardi Gras. At every turn we got glances of curiosity, amusement, sincere happiness at our discovering each other, and verbal expressions that brought tears, appreciation, hilarity, and blessings.

Our friend, Ralph, who had been with a local TV channel but moved to a channel in Philadelphia, sent word that he was going to forego his vacation to Hawaii to avoid missing this memorable occasion. It warmed my heart to hear this. He further added his former local channel would film the affair for him.

Friends and families from other states came, too. Among them was the son of Marvin's deceased brother, Jack (the one wounded shortly after arrival in Korea and responsible for Marvin's hardship discharge). His nephew practiced law in Florida. His wife sat with me at the reunion the day after the wedding, and we spent the time talking about our wonderful Pugh husbands.

My internist at Vanderbilt had previously given her regrets that she could not attend. (That day was going to be celebrated with her husband, because it had been exactly ten years since they married. This was the first time it fell on the day after Thanksgiving the same as on her wedding day.) However, she said she could not resist this special occasion and decided to attend after all.

The reporter and photographer of our story in *The Tennessean* were there. Delores made pictures at every turn to present to us as a wedding present.

Guests were international, representing our friends of different cultures. My grandson, an active military helicopter pilot, came in uniform. Marvin's niece, a Colonel stationed at the Pentagon, but not there that infamous day (9/11), was also at the wedding with her husband, a retired Colonel.

Also present was Frances, from my dentist's office. She teased us by asking if we wanted a fly-over. We knew what she meant. Her son could do it, as he was our President's Marine helicopter pilot in Air Force One at that time.

Two of our high school teachers were there: Miss Brown, the librarian, and "Miss" Dickens, our typing teacher, who later became Mrs. Connelly, after we graduated. In addition, Dr. Raymer, president (since its beginning) of Teresa's and Robin's first college, was also there.

Our precious families and many old friends attended.

It was an indescribable joy to note that two handsome Marines were present to escort our guests and assist wherever needed. They did a marvelous job at every turn. Because it was only two months after 9/11, the music was primarily classical, but patriotic as well.

My son-in-law, Gary, came back to my waiting area where I sat getting last-minute touches and said loudly, "OK. This is your final chance," he teased as he pointed to an escape route through the French doors leading outside. "I gave Marvin the same chance, but he can't run. There are two full-dress Marines up there guarding him. However, you can leap over that stone wall out there and be gone in no time." I laughed at his last-minute "suggestion" and declined his offer to help me flee.

Robin had done a wonderful job orchestrating our wedding. Beautiful flowers adorned the altar and aisle pews, an example of one of the multiple tasks she assumed and completed.

Chris gave me away, walking me (without cane) on his arm from the side entrance, a much shorter walking distance for my convenience. As the processional music began, the audience stood and turned to face the rear of the Church (as was usual for entry of the bride). Then someone noticed that my entry was up front and all turned back to watch me approach the altar. Marvin came from the opposite side, and we were seated in chairs facing Father Peter Whalen. When asked who was giving the bride away, my family responded aloud in unison, "We do."

My face was aglow, because I was so happy. I could not contain my joy, so I smiled through most of the ceremony, wanting to sing with exhilaration. One thing that happened that amused us all nearby (Father Whalen, Deacon Gene Manning and myself) was this high-pitched shrill sound during the singing by the audience. It was unfamiliar to us and the source unknown until Father leaned forward and said something into Marvin's ear. My Honey opened his hand to reveal the uncomfortable hearing aid that he had removed from his ear. (He wore it to ensure that he would hear the marriage vows and respond correctly.)

Later, I was told that all in the audience were either smiling or crying throughout the ceremony. Tears came from my son-in-law, Randy. This was indeed touching to see him weep with mixed emotions. From what I heard later, there were no dry eyes at one time or another during the ceremony. My sons-in-law, Chris and Gary wept, as well. This was particularly noted since all three were not the "crying types."

Veterans and Purple Heart recipients came. Relatives assisted, too. During the ceremony, the Marines stood erect at the side entrances, then behind us as we sat greeting our guests.

This was an unusual informal wedding. After placing the wedding band on my finger, Marvin (certainly not in the "script") kissed both of my hands.

He seldom looked into my eyes for fear of making me giggle. That day, my mind, attitude and spirit were many decades younger than my age. If I ever had been this happy in my life, I could not recall.

To be so completely loved, without condition, was beyond my comprehension. Most importantly, it gave other people the hope that they, too, could also be happy at this advanced age.

The Tennessean reporter, Sylvia Slaughter, did not bring so much as a piece of paper. "Delores and I came because we've grown so attached to you two. We aren't here for a story, we are here to see the wedding."

We had emphasized the wedding was a celebration, but gifts kept arriving anyway. One brown envelope from Delores contained copies of the multiple pictures she had taken for the story.

Among the photos, Robin found a CD bearing a picture like the copy of the newspaper photo showing us kissing. The title bore the same words as the headlines:

"Kisses for Clara." At first she thought it was a compilation of romantic music from the 40s.

She inserted it into the car audio and a man sang, "Kisses for Clara." She learned that he was from Nashville's Music Row, that he and a fellow composer were inspired by our photo, read only that page's contents and wrote the song about and for us. It was thrilling to think strangers, professional song writers, would find our story so outstanding and would take the time to write an original song and record it for us.

Marvin was very pleased, but jested, "My name is not mentioned. I was 'he' all the way through." We were thrilled, pleased and thankful for such an immeasurable gift these young men gave us.

When we felt it was time to exit after the marriage ceremony, Larry took one arm and Marvin the other to steady me. The Marines were very close behind, slowly walking in unison to assure our safety. They opened the double doors coming off the walkway from the parking area, and stood at attention. There awaiting at the driveway was a long, open, white, horse-drawn carriage with a retired Marine in the driver's seat in red coat with his wife beside him dressed in a red tuxedo. Our faces must have registered shock, then smiles, at this unusual sight, prepared as a gift and surprise for us by a fellow Marine.

The Marines slowly closed the doors behind us and in slow cadence kept up with my uncertain steps. Robin explained that the carriage was to take us wherever we wanted to go, courtesy of the drivers (owners). We climbed aboard, with the capable help of those two attentive Marines.

Surrounded by family and well-wishers (Abby, Gogi, Mattie Lou, et al), we chose a ride of a few blocks around the Church area. When we returned, we were greeted by those who had attended the wedding.

Then, off we sped to a local hotel to spend time alone, beginning our honeymoon. We surmised that we had taken all this hoopla in stride and very well, considering our ages. Indeed, we were grateful for all the goodwill and love we had experienced, and especially for each other.

When we returned from our honeymoon, Margit brought us dinner and thanked us for visiting the funeral home when Pop (her husband, chef at the smorgasbord, and dear friend of my family for decades) was there. His death was only two weeks before our marriage. He died in the kitchen of the restaurant, which seemed fitting since he loved it so much. I reminded her of her knowing but questioning quick glance at me that day when Marvin took up his usual stroking of my hand and arm. We both laughed.

"Seeing you two so happy, being at the wedding and knowing the unusual way you two got together, made my grief so much easier to bear," she quietly added.

Our many conversations were replete with stories about our childhoods and always about our North High School and the associated memories: My English teacher, Miss Slonecker; our History teacher, Mrs. Jackson; his Math teacher, Mrs. Sanders; and the fact that our principal, Mr. Noel was our only authority in the school. When he spoke, all listened; he was respected and strictly obeyed. We had something to say about each teacher we had and the influence all had on our characters and how we thought in our later years—the overall effect of our years with them. We always spoke with admiration and respect.

"Marvin, do you remember the old Maxwell House Hotel down on 4th and Church?" I asked during one such session.

"Real well. I used to deliver telegrams there—many of them," he answered.

Wide-eyed and excitedly, I loudly questioned, "You mean you were a real Western Union boy? Wow! I never thought I would meet one in my lifetime and, now, I am married to one. Wow!" He grinned and nodded in the affirmative as I went on. "How old were you? Do you know what an important job you had? That was the only communication some people had. Did you wear that important-looking uniform? Did you ride the bicycle all the time in any kind of weather? Wow! Did you have to ever deliver a 'We regret to inform you… ' telegram?"

To this shower of questions filled with awe, he again simply nodded and grinned at me.

The phone rang. It was Lisa, my youngest daughter. She worked full time as a civilian with Army Recruiting, being sure they had all their needs. The usual mother-daughter information was swapped; then I told her that Marvin and I were talking about old times when we were young. Then after my bragging about him being a Western Union messenger at aged 16, she agreed with my admiration, then suddenly chuckled and asked an off-the-wall question. "Mom, have you ever told him about your mother's biscuit board?" She giggled as she insisted I tell or she would come over and tell him herself. I laughingly promised I would tell him.

"Marvin, when I was about eight years old I did something I never confessed to my Mama or Papa.

"In our back room, which we termed the junk room, my mother hung her big biscuit board that Papa had made by hand. After she made our breakfast biscuits each morning, she dusted the flour from it and hung it back on the butcher paper just outside the kitchen door. One morning as I went into the junk room, I noticed the biscuit board moved slightly. Something was alive behind it. What to do? With my hand, I hit the board as hard as I could to assure me the creature would be dead and, sure enough, a mouse fell dead on the floor. I didn't like rodents, so I left it untouched for someone else to pick up. My mother was the one to discover it. She called to my dad saying there was a dead mouse on the floor under the biscuit board and that he should set some traps in there to get them. Next day, the board moved again, and I zapped it again. Sure enough, another one fell dead. Mama and Papa were puzzled that the traps remained empty, but there was always a dead mouse or two on the floor at odd times. This 'mystery' went on for days, until the biscuit board stopped moving. I assumed I had killed them all," I giggled. "I will never forget the incident.

"Honey, there were some interesting visitors to our apartment when Teresa, Jamian and I lived in the Bellevue area before she went to Dallas to work. She had enrolled again at Belmont, and changed her area of study to computers and business related studies. As always, she befriended the students around her," I said to Marvin.

It was Sunday evening and Marvin and I had just finished our dinner and were completing a crossword puzzle from the Saturday newspaper... a really favorite thing to do together. There had been a question about Arab rulers, refreshing my memory about Teresa and her school friends.

I smiled as I remembered them aloud. "When we had Thanksgiving dinner and other dinners, we would invite some of her friends. Some of them were from Saudi Arabia, others from Venezuela, all over the place (world)—interesting young people, very well-mannered and likeable. One young man from Saudi had an Egyptian mother and a Saudi father. Some of his siblings had businesses in Egypt and twin brothers were going to college in Arizona at the time.

"This young man from Saudi, Medhat, loved my dressing (stuffing) for the turkey and would make a mound of it on his plate at meal time. He always addressed me as Granny or Mother," I reminisced with a smile.

"When Teresa decided on the move to Dallas, she realized I would be alone. One day she came home from school and asked if Medhat could rent a room from me in the apartment. We further discussed it, that he would do his own cooking, since his schedule was so erratic; he could have the guest bathroom, do his own laundry and we could share the living room with the TV. He preferred a 'home' to the dorm, and was delighted with the idea. I seldom heard him come in; his visitors were quiet; it worked out just fine. He had a young doctor visitor who had been his friend in Saudi. He had married an American nurse and stayed here to practice medicine. He was a delight to know. All of his friends were polite and kind.

"Medhat's mother came over to America to see him for a few days, then flew to Arizona to spend some time with the twins. She, too, was extremely personable.

"When Medhat graduated, he returned to Saudi but took a job later at a bank in Switzerland," I added. "He phoned me from Switzerland many times to give regards from his mother. He always wanted to know about my health and how Teresa was doing. If I wasn't home, he chatted with Robin. Medhat seemed like the son I never had. He was constantly asking about our family and came back to Nashville at least half a dozen times, always stopping at Robin's," I said to my patient listener. Now, he knew about Medhat and friends, should I mention them again.

CHAPTER 21

Marvin and I sometimes talked about our children and their lives. On one such day, we were driving down Dickerson Road and approached the area atop the hill where Margit and "Pop" with the other two partners had opened their first restaurant, The Country House. The restaurant had burned after it changed owners a couple of times, and the once well-kept lawn was overgrown with weeds. I was saddened that the quaint white house was no longer there. I recalled aloud how my youngest daughters, Susan and Lisa, had washed tub loads of dishes after school many days and then rushed home to dress to waitress for the dinner hour.

"Susan was a beautiful bride when she married Gary up there (I pointed to the front lawn). My neighbors made her bridal gown, provided the flowers, Margit gave the reception and, therefore, the wedding cost me nothing. It was a neighborhood project in the apartment complex. I shall never forget their kindness.

"Susan was so young. She was to be 17 the next month. The Army had always been Gary's life since an early age, and he retired as a Command Sergeant Major," I said as enthusiastically as I did the first time I boasted about him. "When they transferred to Ft. Sill, Susan drove 100 miles to and 100 miles from pharmacy school every weekday, until she got her degree. I always phoned her when I got a new medicine. Each time I phoned her to ask her opinion about a particular medicine, I called her 'Doctor'. One day when I called her, she said, 'Mom, you may now call me that all the time, because I have now earned my Doctor of Pharmacy.' This was a time to celebrate her hard-earned achievements."

Soon after our marriage, Marvin positioned our kitchen table under the two windows that overlooked the bird feeders and, also, where he planted the popcorn tree his cousin had given us on our honeymoon visit to his Florida home. I could, perhaps, identify about half dozen birds of different species. My knowledge of birds was quite limited. However, I knew I was going to enjoy the feeders and their visitors. Too, Marvin promised to teach me about their habits and to identify them. As we sat by the window one morning I called out in distress as I peered at the activity outside, "Honey, somebody's canary has escaped from its cage." He sat down, hugged my shoulders and chuckled, "That's not a canary; it's a finch." I laughed at myself just as heartily as he did.

When my children complained of subjects at school they didn't perceive as necessary to them, I would always reply, "No knowledge is ever wasted. You will use it at sometime in your life." Marvin agreed with this statement.

Marvin said with a twinkle in his eye, "Let's cruise by the ice cream window, get something really good and go to the park and eat it, while we enjoy the scenery and the people. OK??"

"That's a wonderful idea. I love it."

As our love began to deepen, we seldom wanted to do anything alone—it was always a duo.

At the park that day, we watched the children romp through, some playing tag, others playing with a beach ball, and some just running to and fro. The squirrels ran about, seeking walnuts. Adults were strolling, as they walked their dogs. We chuckled at the ones that appeared to have difficulty keeping up with their frisky companions. We observed a collage of activity as we spooned our treats—chocolate ice cream for me, strawberry and cheesecake for Marvin.

"The other day when Sherrie took me to the doctor, I startled some of the ladies in the office," Marvin chuckled. "Usually, I go in with you, but always with my prostheses on. However, this time, as you remember, the problem was indirectly associated with my stump, so I left my legs off. Sherrie pushed me in—in my wheel chair. The ladies at the check-in counter saw us come in and head toward them. One of the ladies, wide-eyed, clearly moved almost to the point of tears said, 'When did this happen, Mr. Pugh?'

"Korea, l950," was my brief reply,

"All this time... and we didn't know." Her voice quivered.

"Honey, she said that, I bet, with sympathy AND admiration in her voice," I commented. Again, I wanted to hug his neck and smother him with kisses.

In 2006, an incident happened that parents fear most—I lost my first child, Teresa..

She was the daughter that birthed Jamian, and for whom I went to Germany to be his Nanny.

Teresa was extremely intelligent. She was artistic and appreciated all that was beautiful, whether in art, music, decor, small or large landscaping, discussion of ideas, simply put: everything. She chose the military, working in MI (Military Intelligence) and later Electronic Warfare ("Star Wars"). This extended into her civilian life defined as engineering.

When she was experimenting with the "Hippie Movement" in her teen years she distanced herself from me. After some few years, she seemed to come back to me.

She married during the time we owned the Smorgasbord, but they divorced soon after they left the Military. Because Jamian was not happy with his sitters, she asked me to leave Germany and return home to keep him as she further pursued her education. After graduating, she went to Dallas at the request of her Colonel in MI and stayed for several years.

Mothers seem to have extrasensory perception, and mine seemed to sense many things were not right in her life. True, she would not discuss what she did in the military for security reasons and was equally discreet about the jobs that followed. I was unable to delve into her personal life and get firm answers. During these times, I searched for ways to penetrate the wall around her and get some reliable information so that I could hopefully relieve some of the pressure I felt she had on her—but to no avail.

Was this change in her from her younger life or was it from recent times? Was it that in her mind that her father had rejected her by his singling her out for more punishment than her sisters? Was it that her husband had rejected her by divorcing her? She was a genuine "Soccer Mom," excelling in those duties for my grandson. What was the problem (or problems)?

It seemed that every time I phoned her in Dallas, her voice was husky and shaky. My stomach would have a nervous feeling that this was worsening instead of getting better. My impromptu calls caught her off guard, whereas her calls to me were planned and her voice would be clear and normal.

I'm sure she knew I would disagree with whatever pattern she was following, so she never confided in me. But soon, I decided that she had exchanged her moderate occasional drink for steady daily drinking.

She moved back to Nashville, openly drank, neglected her health, refused professional help and developed an infection that took her life.

Her ashes remain in the Columbarium in the Chapel of the Good Shepherd in St. Philip's Episcopal Church adjoining the area where Marvin and I exchanged our vows. God, rest her soul!

"Marvin, let me tell you a funny story about two of my sons-in-law," I said as he rested his head on my lap one evening as we waited for the baseball game to come on. (My youngest daughter, Lisa, had divorced Andre' after a tryst she discovered that he had, and apparently there were others much to our surprise. Then she married Randy.)

One day during a visit to Gary and Susan's by Randy and Lisa, the two men went out behind Gary's house, which adjoined the Army airport, and began to putt some golf balls. Shortly after they started, Randy found a dollar bill. He jubilantly yelled out that he found a dollar on the ground.

"Probably fell from a helicopter, since the guys fly from here," Gary loudly responded. By now they were near the blimp hanger. Gary noted that Randy was still wandering away while looking down at the ground. "You're going to divide your find with me, aren't you?" Gary said in a teasing voice.

"No way," Randy asserted.

Suddenly Randy heard a loud exclamation from Gary. "I just found $20 over there and $20 right here, and over there is another bill—I have to see what it is. I can't believe it. Somehow it surely must have fallen from a helicopter." He jolted toward his right.

They rushed back to the house, excitedly chattering as they both tried to tell Susan and Lisa at the same time about their finds. Gary's total was $90, while Randy found only the single bill.

"You're going to divide with Randy, aren't you?" Lisa asked, expecting a usual positive reply.

"No way. He wouldn't divide a dollar with me." He frowned as he quickly answered.

"Gary, you should divide with him," Susan insisted.

"I would if he hadn't been so stingy with a mere dollar. That'll teach him to divide up." He pretended to be disturbed. This bantered back and forth all afternoon, until time for Randy and Lisa to go home.

A few days later Gary laughingly told Susan and others the truth—that he found no money. It had been planted from his own billfold, however, he wanted to get back at Randy after pretending he wanted half of that small amount. They were constantly playing jokes on one another, and Gary made this ruse linger a little longer so that the family could enjoy the incident.

Lisa resolved to help Randy get "even" at some later date. All who knew the men's individual personalities enjoyed the whole incident when told about it, knowing that Randy would respond in like manner at some time in the future. The family keeps waiting for this hilarious event that's sure to come.

As Marvin and I sat conversing on our front porch one afternoon, he pointed to the city's fire hydrant at the edge of our front yard.

"Let me tell you the story of how I helped change the color of that hydrant a few years ago," he chuckled. I was "all ears," wondering what he meant.

"My neighbor across the street (he pointed to the house to our right) and I were sitting out here talking. Somehow the conversation got changed over to the colors of the fire hydrants," he said.

"Well, I don't think it's fair for the city to paint them all yellow and white. They must be Tennessee fans. Personally, I like Vanderbilt's sports," my neighbor commented.

"I told him I agreed with him. He replied that we could fix it... that our neighbors could keep their preferred colors, but we could change the one in my yard.

"He hurried off to the hardware store and came back with two cans of spray paint—one was black and the other gold. I sprayed with one color, and he sprayed with the other, until we felt it was just right."

(By this time I was laughing, remembering that in my lifetime, no one touched city property that I knew...)

Marvin went on to say that no one in the neighborhood had commented to him about the color change.

About four weeks passed and one day he looked out the door and saw a city waterworks car with a man inside, writing something and also looking at the hydrant. The man stayed for more than twenty minutes; however, Marvin did not know when he first arrived. Three days later, a crew of two came out and painted the hydrant back to the original colors of yellow and white.

When his brother-in-law, Woody, and wife, Laura, came by for a visit about three months later, Marvin complained to Woody about the change back to yellow and white. Well, Woody told Marvin he would take care of it and forthwith went to the hardware store and alone painted it back to Marvin's preferred colors. However, he painted only half of it, which was all right with Marvin; half being fair and equal.

Within a few weeks, Marvin went out to see it painted again as it originally was—yellow and white all over.

Somehow Woody's brother (an employee of the fire department) on being told about the episode, informed them that one color denoted the end of the line and the other was the water pressure there. (Fortunately, no one was fined.)

This incident caught my son-in-law's attention. I believe it's amused everyone with whom Gary plays golf.

One Christmas, we were graced with this beautiful and profound card, handwritten and composed by Marvin's daughter, Sherrie. It read:

> *A family is like a patchwork quilt.*
> *Many varied pieces coming together*
> *to make a beautiful work of art.*
>
> *You are two of those beautiful patches in our family quilt,*
> *and I wish you peace and love this Christmas*
> *and in the new year.*
> *—Love, Sherrie*

Among the gifts that also came from Sherrie, shortly after the above card was received, was a quilted heart-shaped, handmade ornament for the tree. On her next day visit, I inquired as to what inspired such a lovely card. She replied that as she stood in line at the store to check out her items, she studied the various prints in her materials and jotted down her thoughts about her purchase.

"Marvin, do you remember how 'lean' our Christmas used to be when we were young?" He nodded and smiled. "I usually hung my stocking and got a peppermint candy cane, an apple and an orange in it. Oranges were a treat; they were rare. Anyway, I usually woke up to a tea set of tin dishes, which consisted of two tiny cups, two tiny saucers and two plates, a little larger than the saucers (cost about .29 cents at the five-and-dime store), and a baby doll with cloth body stuffed with cotton (cost about $1.29). Shirley Temple dolls were the rage then, the dream of every little girl, but they cost about $10. The nearest I got was a doll with blond hair, stuffed body, but her eyes would close when I lay her down. Cost was about $2.29; but this satisfied me since she had hair and looked about my age," I added, remembering so well.

He chuckled as he answered, "I usually got just the stocking with a piece of candy, an orange and an apple. That was it."

"Our decorations always consisted of two small wreaths for the front room. We had shades that pulled up and down, and Mama would put the wreath on the ring in the center of the shade. That was the sum of our decorations. However, one Christmas, my brother, Buster, who had a job as "Drug Store cowboy" (this is what he called himself, because he delivered prescriptions every afternoon on his bike for the drug store, and also groceries for the store across the street) brought home a real live cedar tree. We bought lights (the big bulb kind then), a few ornaments, and some metallic material that hung down as ice. Remember them?" He nodded and laughed again.

Marvin could not recall ever having a tree. Then we talked about when the commercials used to be just talking, not music or singing. And how the first television was black and white, limited to one channel, and how the picture would go around until we got it tuned properly.

We changed our talk then to different subjects, all varied. I recalled one. Prior to my marriage to Marvin, I lived with my daughter, Robin, and her husband, Chris. Next door was a young couple. Their house was on the corner, therefore, we could look down upon their back deck from our kitchen window. Our front faced the other street off their street.

They were childless, but that changed. In a few months, Michael Moe was born. Since both parents worked, Robin asked if we could babysit him. They agreed. We were pleased, since Robin, too, was childless. So, within a couple months or so, we began the pleasure of keeping him every weekday. His parents addressed him as Michael, but Robin and I preferred to call him Moe. Soon, our choice caught on, and all called him Moe.

As he grew, he did many things that brought joy to us. One was his habit of when waking up from a nap he pounded on the wall beside his bed. Many times we left the bedroom door ajar, but knew he had rather pound to get Robin's response (which was most entertaining to me, too). He would be standing, holding on to his bed rail or lying on his back. She would rush in and extend her arms while humbly bowing several times muttering, "Yes, Master. I am here. What do you wish?" When he was just past three, his sister, Lesley, was born. We were given the joy of keeping her for some time, too. We were invited to celebrate Moe's Bar Mitzvah when he was 13 years old, and three years later, Lesley's Bat Mitzvah. Though not blood-related, they have brought pleasure to Robin, Chris, and me.

CHAPTER 22

One day as we sat watching the birds at our two feeders, a favorite pastime that almost all enjoyed who visited Marvin and me, I commented with laughter about the piano music coming from the TV.

"Honey, I actually owned a piano at one time. The maiden teacher at the end of the street—remember the brick house and the next door yellow brick that shared a view of Madison from Sixth Avenue?" He nodded and smiled, knowing well that I had a lengthy story to tell to go with the piano information.

"Miss Baumbach lived with an elderly couple—interesting people—in the brick house. Her landlord was at that time, from what I heard, Nashville's leading photographer, taking posed pictures that took time. He was German and very interesting." I mused upon remembering. Marvin smiled at my momentary hesitation.

"Many times I would be on my front porch and hear her play the piano and sing. The piano was by the open window. Remember, no air conditioning in those days!! She was a music teacher at my school, and she had a 'trained' voice—hitting the high notes with control. Sometimes, she would invite me in and would play as I would sing, critiquing me as I sang for her," I added, as he listened patiently.

"The next summer she told me her piano was for sale. I excitedly rushed home and told Papa and within the week the piano was being rolled down the street to go into my house. The total cost was $15 and that included the cost of the two helpers. It was found to have some defects—ivory missing from some of the keys, half a dozen or so keys with no sound when hit, and a couple of keys out of tune... but it looked good to me... enough keys working on the piano to allow me to take music for a new song and memorize the melody. I learned to avoid the 'bad keys,'" I giggled as I recalled my love for that old relic. Marvin laughed at my story.

Then I became serious as I reflected further on my mid teens. "That old relic brought to mind a sad time in my life, too. After Mama had her first stroke, her body exhibited the harshness of her disabilities. Her eyes did not look the same way—when she looked at me with the left eye, her right went to another direction; after she learned to walk she dragged her right leg with each step; her speech was slurred and difficult to understand; and her crippled right arm and hand could not hold onto anything."

I further recalled her severe illness and Marvin admonished me, asking me to change the subject, but I so wanted to let him know, "Her mind was not right. Dr. Hal came every week, but to no real avail. He warned me that stroke victims sometimes turned on the one they cared for the most. I told him about her 'temper fits' that seemed to have no reasoning. In essence, he said we could only do our best with her.

"If I took a few minutes a day to play my piano (to escape), she would grab the lid over the keys and try to slam it down on my fingers. This was so harsh to come from the mother who had kissed me without fail (except for once) to send me off to school... the mother who had faithfully nursed me through sickness... and on and on... Sometimes she would lash out at me for no reason with her left hand, trying to get to my eyes or my face. My only response was to hold her wrists until she simmered down. Each day was a challenge to me, and my prayers to God were constant as I tried to figure out my situation."

Marvin took both my hands in his and said, "Chick-a-dee (a pet name for me), you always boost me up when you think I'm sad, so let this matter ride! OK? You only upset yourself and me when you refer to the past, and you really hurt yourself. It does no good to remember those days of your past." He then put his arms around me and hugged me tightly to him.

"Pooh (Pugh) Bear (I often affectionately called him by this nickname), I love you so very much. Thank you for listening to me rattle on. You are so very patient with me when I recall the past."

The next day, as we sat again by the kitchen window, I mentally reflected on my sadness of the previous day and observed verbally as many times before, "Marvin, you amaze me that you are not bitter that both of your legs are missing. You are truly my hero. How you came through all that you have and not lost your sanity is beyond me. What would we in this country do without the likes of you?" He looked into my eyes for a bit as if about to say something and looked away.

Frowning, he looked at me intently and talked, "Bitterness about my physical condition is not a part of my life. Divine Providence carried me from the first place and on to the others. I firmly believe that Angels watched over me. My survival was not of my doing."

"Do you know the thought occurred to me that if both of us had not had leg problems we would not have gone to the School Reunion that night where we celebrated our 55th Reunion? Though we lived a few years in the same neighborhood within a couple of blocks we never met before. We don't remember seeing each other except when you returned from WWII to finish high school and we vaguely remember that period of time," I added.

"Indeed. Pat kept after me to attend as Korean veterans were being cited, and you came only because that dude you remembered slightly surely would be on crutches or in a wheel chair and nobody would notice that you got about on a walker," he laughed.

"Yeah, and Mattie Lou was responsible for me. She kept calling me to attend, but I refused, saying I didn't want to see my friends while walking with support. Just one of us not showing up that night would have meant we probably never would have met again. Imagine that!!

"Divine Providence again," I laughed heartily with a happy song-feeling.

Knowing what a fortunate woman I was to be loved by him, I pulled my chair close to him and lay my head on his shoulder. Soon, I was cupping his precious face in my hands and smothering him with kisses. How many times a day do I kiss him? This lady cannot accurately say, but they are numerous.

Marvin very much liked to sit on the couch and watch baseball on television. When a game came on, I would busy myself with doing something else. One day I decided that joining him was the best idea for that day. So I sat quietly beside him, occasionally giving him a kiss or resting my head on his lap. Shortly, I began to watch the activity with interest.

When commercials would come on, I felt I could comment or ask questions such as, "How did that fellow get on base two?"

His amused reply was, "It's called second base—like first, second, and third base, not one, two and three. OK? And he got it by stealing—running when the other guys weren't looking."

He pointed, "That's the shortstop, the left fielder, the right fielder. You'll learn as you go, if you really want to watch them with me," he said as he straightened his couch throw pillow. He seemed pleased that I intended to join him and learn the game.

"Honey, I went to several ball games at Sulphur Dell, but could only recognize a home run. I think I only went to watch the people or socialize with my friends. I never knew about scores and such," I laughed.

A few weeks went by. Marvin was pleased with my growing knowledge of the game and ability to recognize the players.

"Can you imagine that I had the privilege, along with Robin, of going to two professional base ball games as guests of Ralph's in Pennsylvania when we were selling the Blumen Box? Yes, indeed! We were guests at a Cincinnati Reds game, sitting in choice seats and, then after the game, we sat in the waiting area of their locker rooms. Outside were fans waiting patiently for autographs. When we went out and crossed over to where they waited, some of the kids approached Ralph for an autograph. He laughingly said, 'You don't want my autograph—I'm nobody. I'm not a player.' With this statement, they parted like the Red Sea—I like to express a reaction like that," I giggled.

"Oh, oh, Sweetheart, let me tell you the best part. I got a baseball out of my visit, and everyone on the team signed it—even the signature of Pete Rose... I think that was his last year to manage. I saw Mrs. Rose in the area with us, too. To think, I wasn't knowledgeable enough to appreciate a great game and to top it all off, the signed baseball." I sighed with disappointment.

"Within a short time, we were guests watching the St. Louis Cardinals, too." I cheerfully added.

Since we could only get certain games on TV, they all became my favorites, but he told me we had to follow one team to really make it enjoyable—and that one became the Atlanta Braves. I began to give them nick names: The shortstop (Furcal) was a ballet dancer when he twirled to catch the ball, then twirl again to throw it to first. McCann became Baby Huey to me because he looked chubby, and had such an innocent face. Another player was Texarcano, because we had difficulty spelling and pronouncing his name. He played excellent first base one year.

Another thing we began to share and enjoy from the beginning was to solve the crypto/word games in the daily newspaper after breakfast and the newspaper's crossword puzzle during the evening meal. Marvin is good at providing the answer to the "guy stuff" problem-questions such as geography, tools, mechanical parts, and "stuff" girls don't necessarily find interesting. He depends on me for the last word in spelling, musical terms, names and other words not as knowledgeable to him. We look forward to the next paper, mainly for sports and the puzzles.

Once I asked him how he became so interested in crossword. He answered, "When I was in the Marines in WWII—no dictionary was handy, so when I ran across a new word or one I wasn't sure of, I would write it in a little notebook I had for future reference."

I was impressed by this and told him so.

Often, we spoke of both wars, especially Korea. One day, he told me of being a member of an FO team in the Inchon and Seoul areas. "I was a Forward Observer," he said. "What's that?" I whispered. He replied that meant he went out alone or with a team to secure the way for his fellow Marines. "My FO team was attached to an infantry company to spot enemy targets. The radio operator's duty was to inform the artillery battery of the target to be destroyed so that the infantry could move in and get less resistance. One day we were out of contact range of the infantry moving in and could not fire. They sent me for verbal contact with the infantry to find out where and when to fire." His voice trailed away.

My voice quivered as I asked, "You mean you went out there alone with that many enemy in the area? With only a rifle—alone? Wow! That reminds me of how I was glad I was a girl when I watched the news reels in the movie theaters when WWII was going on. You guys would hit the water and then wade in to the beach to gunfire that didn't seem to miss. I would cover my eyes and weep inside. How horrible it seemed, beyond description—."

Later, when the Marines moved to North Korea, he was transferred to an artillery battery. Marvin was instructed on how to fire the lo5 Howitzer. This was his assignment until he began his journey home.

At this time, I changed the subject. "Honey, your Marine mascot is a bulldog, isn't it? I know—once a Marine, always a Marine. When you were so young—healthy—robust, you were really of bulldog status, but now, you're my precious Chihuahua/Bulldog. That's your new nickname to go along with Honey, Sweetheart, and the other pet names I call you." I chuckled.

"We're older now and not so robust anymore." I stood behind him, hugged him as he sat in his wheelchair. Then I leaned over to get some good "sugar." He was indeed my hero and love.

Spring is here. The loveliest time of the year to me. I once wrote: Spring is like the newness of life; a new beginning. The trees are coming alive, flowers are blooming, birds singing, the promise of hummingbirds returning. The Summer will follow: Fullness of life, in full bloom.

The popcorn tree that Marvin's cousin gave us, when we visited him during our honeymoon in Florida, has grown from a tiny plant to be an enormous tree. On inquiry, we learned that this tree was brought to the United States by Benjamin Franklin and is known as a

Chinese tallow tree. It grows better in warm southern states; however, Marvin and I wanted the challenge of growing it here. Very much as our marriage, it persists against all odds.

Each winter, visitors will comment that the tree looks dead. I insist that it be given "another year," because I believe it will survive. The cold zero degree weather with its blistery winds toss it to and fro, but it withstands bravely. When Spring arrives, the other trees produce leaves, but our "honeymoon tree" stands barren. (Will this be the year that the critics will be right?)

I visually inspect the tree each morning from the kitchen window when we sit for breakfast and watch the outside activity. The little birds jump about from limb to limb and then settle to eat from the feeders and fly away. Sometimes, the squirrels mount the barren limbs and jump over onto the bird feeders to get sustenance after or during the feathered guests visits. Their "gymnast-like" dexterity never ceases to amaze us—always a new and difficult way to enter the bird feeders again.

One Spring morning we will find green pods hanging from the popcorn tree and, another day, we will see the popcorn-like blooms being eaten by the birds. Joyously, we survey the single base that grew upward and divide into two strong sections with roots that travel strongly far from the base of the tree. Just as Marvin and I, the tree continues to survive from roots (our roots being love and marriage as one) that grow longer and stronger each year.

We believe that Divine Intervention brought Marvin out of Korea and home to his family, walked me through tribulations and finally brought us together. SHALOM.

God is Love, and I Corinthians 13 describes fully His intentions for us all.